Bloom's Modern Critical Views

Bloom's Modern Critical Views

Bloom's Modern Critical Views

MILAN KUNDERA

Edited and with an introduction by
Harold Bloom
Sterling Professor of the Humanities
Yale University

CHELSEA HOUSE
PUBLISHERS
A Haights Cross Communications Company
Philadelphia

Library of Congress Cataloging-in-Publication Data

Milan Kundera / edited and with an introduction by Harold Bloom.
     p. cm. -- (Bloom's modern critical views)
Includes bibliographical references.
     ISBN: 0-7910-7043-3

Chelsea House Publishers
1974 Sproul Road, Suite 400
Broomall, PA 19008-0914

http://www.chelseahouse.com

Contributing Editor: Aaron Tillman

Cover designed by Terry Mallon

Cover photo by Fridrik Rafussion; courtesy of Harper Collins

Layout by EJB Publishing Services

Contents

Editor's Note

My Introduction meditates upon the literary status of *The Unbearable Lightness of Being*. Like the rest of Kundera, it already may be a Period Piece.

Robert C. Porter describes Kundera's early cycle of love stories, after which Pearl Kazin Bell praises Kundera for his transitions from history to autobiography.

For Peter Kussi, Kundera has the distinction of "a dialogue with truth." More soberly, the critic John Bayley gives us a balanced estimate, weighing the novelist's skills against his authentic limitations.

Kundera's erotic obsessions are admired by Mark Sturdivant, while Roger Kimball finds an affinity between Kundera and the poet, W. H. Auden.

Terry Eagleton, a Marxist cheerleader, grants Kundera "formidable strength," after which the superb fabulist Italo Calvino expresses some ironic reservations in regard to Kundera's view of kitsch.

In Ellen Pifer's judgement, Kundera turns the art of narration against itself in *The Book of Laughter and Forgetting*, while James S. Hans considers the aesthetics of *The Unbearable Lightness of Being*.

Laughable Loves is seen by Michael Carroll as a valid instance of cyclic form, after which John O'Brien emphasizes the author's overt role throughout Kundera's work.

Tom Wilhelmus finds Nietzsche's Eternal Return in *The Joke*, while Vicki Adams concludes this volume by celebrating Kundera's Post-Modernism.

Introduction

Prague's Velvet Revolution of November 1989 was a great event in political liberation, and is part of the sequence that culminated in the transfer of power from Gorbachev to Yeltsin in the winter of 1991, which marked the formal end of the Soviet Union. Milan Kundera exiled himself from Prague to France in 1975, and has maintained considerable critical prestige down to the present moment, in 2002. I have just reread *The Unbearable Lightness of Being* for the first time since its initial publication in 1984, when it seemed to me a work of some accomplishment. I had not reread it a decade later, when I included it in the listing at the end of my book, *The Western Canon*. Uncertain whether I would find a canonical candidate in it now, I wonder seriously if it is one more Period Piece.

Kundera acknowledges Laurence Sterne and Denis Diderot as specific ancestors, and I suppose he might add Hermann Broch, as well as the inevitable Kafka, and Robert Musil. With such precursors, he is dwarfed. *The Unbearable Lightness of Being* is formulaic, over-determined, and in places unbearably light. In 1989, Italo Calvino praised the book for its storytelling art, and for emulating Sterne and Diderot in spontaneity. But Calvino had less use for Kundera's category of kitsch:

> ... to see the absolute contrast with kitsch in the image of a naked woman wearing a man's bowler hat does not seem to me totally convincing.

The distinguished English critic John Bayley praises Kundera's best-known novel for its old-fashioned art, and for carrying through a Nietzschean distinction between "lightness of being" and "weight":

Lightness of being is associated with the author's voice, with the cinema and sex, with irresponsibility and definition, with politics. Weight or heaviness of being, on the other hand, is associated with love and fidelity, suffering, chance, fiction, form and content ... death.

I can agree with Bayley that this is a perfectly workable formula, but it stales with repetition. Aside from its narrative verve, *The Unbearable Lightness of Being* depends upon the relationship between the womanizing Tomas and the selfless, loving Tereza. Can Kundera render this fresh, or is it totally similar to many stories we all of us have read and known?

Philip Roth, who admired Kundera, has in common with the Czech novelist only the frequently non-ironic conviction that achieved sexuality can be an aesthetic fulfillment it if is represented with sufficient skill. The Roth of *Sabbath's Theater* sustains this problematic conviction; Kundera, I fear, does not. Roth has a zest, learned from Shakespeare, that begins to convert into meaning through Sabbath's excess of being, a Falstaffian drive for more life. Kundera's Tomas, the "epic womanizer," has considerable comic self-understanding, but lacks Sabbath's Falstaffian exuberance.

The "Prague Moment" has gone by; young people no longer go off to the Czech capital with Kundera in their back-packs. I cannot think that Kundera much relishes being praised as another Post-Modernist; he is aware that Cervantes outdoes everyone at the art of the self-conscious novel. I end, as I began, in some doubt as to Kundera's lasting eminence. Much talent has been invested, ere this, in what proved to be Period Pieces.

ROBERT C. PORTER

"Freedom is my Love": The Works
of Milan Kundera

Between 1963 and 1968 Kundera produced ten short love stories, which depict the comic as well as the tragic side of human relations. In 1970 eight of them appeared in a collected edition, the author having decided to omit two which he had come to regard as weak. Examining the original ten stories we find in them a philosophical progression which is taken up and developed in the novels.

An article by Milan Blahynka (*Plamen* no. I, 1967) discusses at length the first two volumes and discovers in them a system of theses and antitheses; the first three stories are concerned with a hero, frustrated in love and forced to deceive others. A young man is in love with a beautiful singer who refuses to requite his love, so he has a friend pose as an impresario, the fake impresario falls in love with her, but cannot reveal his true identity or his love, and the hero remains frustrated—the girl he loves has lost her heart to a man who does not exist. The second story involves a young composer pouring out his heart into a piece of music for the girl he loves; but she finds the composition false and insincere, not knowing that she is the inspiration for it. To compound the irony, her husband writes poetry which the musician finds false and insincere, but she and her husband actually write it between them. The third story concerns a young university lecturer in Prague. The young man is badgered by the author of a worthless publication to write a

From *Index on Censorship*, Vol. 4, No. 4, Winter, 1975. Reprinted in Short Story Criticism, Vol. 24. © 1975 by Index on Censorship.

review of it. But the lecturer is reluctant to do so because he feels the work is so bad—and yet he lacks the moral courage to tell the man so. Anyway, he has suffered at the hands of publishers himself. Finally, to get rid of the persistent author he accuses him of making sexual advances to his girlfriend. This merely brings the author's strong-willed and indignant wife into the action. The result is that the young lecturer loses his job, his flat and his girlfriend.

In each story the love is sincere and yet it is either doomed from the start, or becomes more hopeless by the heroes' attempts to deceive others, to control their lives and thus to enhance their own happiness. In the first story, 'I, a mournful god,' the hero/narrator actually tells us:

> I don't write, I live, and speaking frankly, I despise authors of events on paper, I despise them for the sweaty describers of life they are. On the other hand, I venerate authors of events lived in life—I count myself amongst these. There are two kinds of people in life: authors of life and puppets of life.

This sums up the thesis of the first three stories. All three heroes try to be authors of life and are hoist with their own petard.

In the second volume we have an antithesis. In these three stories the heroes are more or less satisfied in love, or in their love adventures, but insist on tampering with the emotion. The best of these stories has appeared in English under the title 'A game of make-believe' (*New Writing in Czechoslovakia*, Penguin 1969). A young couple are on a motoring holiday, alone together for the first time. The girl pretends to be a hitch-hiker, the man picks her up and readily falls into the role of lecherous motorist. The game escalates and results in the girl acting the part of a whore and becoming completely divorced from her former self:

> The girl's sobs soon turned into crying out loud, and she kept repeating that pitiful tautology countless times: 'I am me, I am me, I am me ...'

The young man had to summon sympathy to his aid (he had to summon it from a long way off, for there was none near by), to try and quiet the girl. They still had thirteen days of their holiday left.

If the first volume of stories shows the authors of other people's lives failing, their conceit getting its just deserts, volume two shows that people are not even the authors of their own lives, for even when all is going well between two human beings a new dimension may suddenly emerge, a game may become too real, a joke become a tragedy.

The third volume, however, presents us with a synthesis. Man, unable to control others' lives, and then unable to control his own, must come to terms with the world and with what freedom he has. There were originally four stories in this volume: 'Let the old dead make way for the young dead,' 'Symposium,' 'Edward and God' and 'Doctor Havel ten years later.' Each of these stories involves people making their peace with the contradictions in human relationships. They may well discover new elements in themselves and others; they may well decide that complete happiness and requited love are illusions; they may realise the limitations on their own freedom; and yet there is, at the end of the day, a feeling of contentment and assurance which is sought after in vain in the two earlier volumes.

The title 'Symposium' has its original meaning here—'drinking together.' In a provincial hospital a group of doctors and nurses are on night duty, drinking and discussing women. Doctor Havel is a notorious womaniser. We see in this character an example of contentment and perhaps resignation in the face of paradox and even defeat: Havel tells us that his greatest success with women concerned his being rejected once by a girl who usually slept with anybody—obviously, he argues, he must have been something special for her! One character, Elizabeth, nearly gases herself and we do not know if it is accidental, or a genuine suicide attempt. Several theories are advanced, but no one truth emerges. Certainly, she was keen to seduce Havel and failed—as he says himself—'I refused Elizabeth precisely because I don't know how to be free. Not sleeping with Elizabeth is in fashion.'

The main event in the story is tragic—someone nearly dies: and yet from this all the characters derive a certain satisfaction. Flejs man is happy in his belief that Elizabeth attempted to take her life for love of him; Elizabeth herself gains precisely the romantic kudos she lacked at the beginning of the story. And yet true motives are not revealed and in emotional terms, the characters resolve very little. Significantly, the last chapter is entitled (in English) 'Happy End.'

'Edward and God' concerns a young teacher who starts going to church in order to impress and ultimately seduce his devout girlfriend. He gets into trouble at school for going to church, his girlfriend hears of his persecution and bestows her favours on him as a reward for his faith. Edward suffers from pangs of conscience, returns to church, the face of God appears before him and: 'Look! Yes! Edward is smiling. He is smiling and his smile is a happy one ...' Again the contradictions that beset human relationships are faced up to and the result, if not happiness, is at least contentment.

The final synthesis in this cycle of short stories is emphasised by the presentation of the 1970 edition. Two of the weaker stories were omitted—one from volume one and one from volume two; one of the stories from volume two was shifted to volume one and one from volume three to volume two. This rearrangement would seem to strengthen the thesis (deception) in volume one, the antithesis (self-deception) in volume two and the synthesis in volume three.

The final synthesis is realised by the increasing sophistication of humorous devices throughout the stories. The comic element in the earlier stories is, on the whole, based on irony, especially ironic incidents of the characters' own making—quite simply, things done in spite never turn out right. The result is to alienate the characters one from the other whilst at the same time allowing the reader to sympathise with and understand all. In 'Symposium' a fuller range of comic devices is brought into play—bathos, bawdry, puns, and more especially, 'comic visuality.' The story is broken up into 36 very short chapters bearing titles apparently plagiarised from the silent film e.g. 'A call for help,' 'The doctor's theory,' 'The uncertainty of all things,' 'Happy end.' The overall effect is to speed up the action and make it seem 'jerky,' yet the events of the story are all perfectly rational and even everyday. There is no embroidery and no hint of the grotesque.

PEARL K. BELL

The Real Avante-Garde

Novels of protest against oppression and injustice have invariably taken the form of brutal realism, from a Zola to a Solzhenitsyn, since they seek to document horrors with a wealth of detail and fact. But questions of form apart, since the realistic novel is an old form, how long can one go on piling detail on detail, in a mounting demonstration of evil? Writers of protest have tried other modes, such as satire, yet satire requires that a reader have more than a passing knowledge of the facts about an inhumane regime. (How can anyone lacking intimate knowledge of the Soviet Union, for example, fully appreciate the cunning ingenuity and deadly accuracy of Alexander Zinoviev's satirical assault on Soviet society in *The Yawning Heights*?) Other writers, preeminently Kafka, have given us a sense of the individual's helplessness against incomprehensible authority through surreal abstractions of reality: one remembers *In the Penal Colony*, and the terrible machine that slowly executes the condemned by tattooing his sentence on his back. More recently, principally from writers who have lived and suffered through the experience of Communist regimes, there has come a new form which might be called the literature of compression.

This kind of imaginative writing about the world of Eastern Europe attempts to convey the airless, claustrophobic nature of its life by condensing the conventional apparatus of character, action, and judgment into a small

From *Commentary*, Vol. 70, No. 6, December, 1980. © 1980 by *Commentary*.

and heightened span. It suggests visual actuality with fragmented images and shreds of shadowy detail rather than capacious description, and conveys the writer's loathing of his rulers in oblique metaphors rather than demonstrative statements....

What undoubtedly accounts in part for the self-limitation of such writing is not only the infamous hypocrisy of socialist realism, which prettifies and denies the truth, but the unnatural degree of vigilance that nonconforming writers under Communism must maintain if they have any instinct for literary and physical survival without capitulation. To live under the shutters of threat deprives a writer of all patience for the cumulative pace and casual clutter of conventional narratives that stop to linger over the color of a woman's eyes or the cut of her clothes.

A writer like Milan Kundera ... seems, even after he settled in the West, to be driven by nervous urgency, a sense of dwindling time. He has small tolerance for the voluminous recreation of surface appearances because the minatory ghost of history constantly reminds him that the real world is brutally unlike the way it looks. In Kundera's new novel, *The Book of Laughter and Forgetting*, ... dancers in a circle become the symbolic image of the ideological power of Communism. A circle which magically protects the true believer from the perils of skepticism is also a circle that suffocates the individual dancers in a closed ring of solidarity.... In the five novels of Milan Kundera which have so far been published in the United States, we can trace the path of the dissident writer: from protest, to comedy and satire, to surrealist compression. (p. 66)

More polemical and expansive than anything Kundera has written since, *The Joke* is a straightforward political narrative (greatly enriched, however, by the author's psychological acumen) exposing the excesses of the Czech inquisitors during the Stalinist years....

It seems safe to guess that by the time he finished [this] anti-Stalinist protest novel, Kundera had grown so weary of the Marxist kitsch pouring out of every loudspeaker in Czechoslovakia that he wanted to banish politics from his fiction altogether....

Most of the stories in *Laughable Loves* crackle with irony, but the comic entanglements of his characters are so precisely observed, and related with such a winning air, that in the end this Czech *La Ronde* is touching as well as funny. Kundera has none of Schnitzler's world-weary cynicism about sex, and he seems determined to show that there is just as much erotic jealousy, narcissism, promiscuity, and absurdity in a Communist society as there is in decadent capitalist countries and a good thing, too. Even when sex turns to farce under Kundera's sardonic scrutiny, it remains a solacing basis of disorder in an ironclad life. What he slyly sets out to demonstrate is that even though socialist realism is too high-principled to be bothered with the sexual diversions of everyday life, he finds sex entirely worthy of literary attention, whether he is mocking a paunchy Casanova long past his prime or a couple of frantic Lotharios so easily distracted by new quarries that they never consummate any campaign of seduction.

Though Kundera is astringently anti-romantic, his laughter is not mean-spirited nor his irony scornful. In *Laughable Loves* he is no longer protesting a ruthless political system, but looking with canny amusement at that enigmatic and quirky arena of desire shared by all of humankind. (p. 67)

[*Life is Elsewhere*] moves farther away from the conventions of realistic fiction than anything Kundera had written earlier.... It is clear that in this mordant portrait of the artist. Kundera was satirizing the cultural infantilism with backwardness that he sees as endemic to Czechoslovakia and whose most pervasive symptom is the lyrical approach to life and politics....

The Czech passion for lyrical poetry, Kundera believes, is a sign of puerility because such poetry is a realm in which any statement is immediately accorded veracity. During the Stalinist years, this poetic enthusiasm induced a general haze of gullibility and innocence that blinded the Czechs to the reality of a world in which people were being jailed and tormented, and this seems to be the object of Kundera's satire. Unfortunately his contempt for the Czech devotion to lyric poetry never acquires convincing satiric clarity in *Life is Elsewhere*, at least not for readers unfamiliar with the peculiarities of Czechoslovakia's cultural and political development and thus unable to respond intelligently to the novel's complex motivation....

On the surface *The Farewell Party* pretends to be nothing more than a light-hearted romp about a philandering jazz trumpeter and his Machiavellian scheme for shedding a pregnant mistress. But the spa is soon revealed to be a bizarre microcosm of the world at large, complete with comic saints and righteous sinners, disenchanted politicians and jealous wives.

With great agility, Kundera packs an extraordinary variety of moods and genres into this short and ostensibly inconsequential jest: bedroom farce, romantic love, melodrama, high comedy of manners, philosophical rumination. It is a ballet of incongruities, and as such would seem to be Kundera's celebration of life as disorder, which thrives only in freedom.... Though the word Communism never appears in this novel, and the spa seems to exist in cloud-cuckoo land, Kundera's pretense of comic inconsequence is undercut by the kind of pointed intelligence that is all the more affecting for being so offhand.

What is immediately striking about [*The Book of Laughter and Forgetting*] ... is the bold authority that has enabled him to work out a genuinely innovative way of expressing, not representing, the reality of his past life in his homeland. He has completely rejected the traditional, by now well-worn and creatively unprofitable ways of writing about inhumanity and exile, and has drawn instead on the vitality of the unexpected and the concentrated imagery ordinarily found in poetry. It is a difficult and demanding book, which is not to say that Kundera indulges in the feckless obscurity of synthetic modernism, but neither is he willing to ease the reader's task. His fantasy requires a willingness to suspend the expectations we bring to realistic narrative.

Though Kundera calls his book a novel in the form of variations, it is more accurately read as a group of stories loosely connected by the elegiac and sardonic meditations of the author on his past and the imperatives of memory. The elusiveness of memory, and the compulsion it becomes for those who must live in exile, is a central theme.... Though so much of Kundera's rumination about his former life in *The Book of Laughter and Forgetting* is drenched in the poisonous spume of East European politics, he poignantly conveys how the sorrow of exile from one's homeland, even though life there had become intolerable, is an inescapable price of freedom. (p. 68)

The boldness with which Kundera cuts back and forth among the different levels from history to autobiography to the apparition of soaring angels transfigures the familiar with a power entirely his own. Through this triumphant act of the imagination, Kundera has made his experience of non-being an ineradicable part of our consciousness.

One returns from Milan Kundera to our own middle-class world. Our lives, we are told, are empty and meaningless, we have been dehumanized by false gods. The American writers who believe this wearily strain to convey their radical message with the experimental tricks of exhausted modernism, in order to assert that they are the cultural avant-garde. Yet how feeble their gestures seem alongside the writers who are driven to take genuine literary risks out of the necessity of expressing a reality that is literally, physically dehumanizing.

If there is an avant-garde today, it is to be found not in the technical acrobatics of Western writers, but among the dissident novelists and poets of

Communist Europe. The freshness and strength of their innovations come not from their political dissent but from the fact that, having experienced the actuality of concentration camps, prison, and exile, they are driven by the need to find a new voice for old horrors. (p. 69)

PETER KUSSI

Milan Kundera: Dialogues with Fiction

Milan Kundera writes fiction in order to ask questions. Could that have actually happened? Why was he so ashamed of her anyway? Then why did he make it all up? Why did he lie? Why is she so nervous? Has Mirek ever understood her? These questions, part of a dialogue between narrator and reader, or perhaps between narrator and author, are taken from the first pages of Kundera's latest novel [*The Book of Laughter and Forgetting*].... (p. 206)

Kundera interrogates his characters, poses questions to his various narrator-personae, engages his readers and puzzles them into questioning themselves. He is after clarity, definition, with a French faith in lucidity and a Czech mistrust of absolutes. The devil laughs at God because of His inscrutability; angels laugh with God at the simplicity of creation. Kundera, with an ironic smile, constructs fictional worlds in which patient investigation by narrator, characters and readers is rewarded by glimpses into the rules of the game.

Kundera is an astonishingly inventive author who uses a variety of structural ways to question his themes.... [In *The Joke*] he used the technique of multiple narration. By cross-examining the accounts of the story furnished by four narrators, Kundera exposed their overlapping delusions, to use the memorable phrase of critic Elizabeth Pochoda [see CLC, Vol. 19]. In prewar

From *World Literature Today*, Vol. 57, No. 2, Spring, 1983. © 1983 by *World Literature Today*.

13

Czech literature this technique was favored by Karel Capek. But whereas Capek the relativist showed that each man has his own truth, Kundera the skeptic shows that each man has his own falsehood.

A related technique employed by Kundera is the multiple point of view on the author's part, resulting in shifts of perspective and of the relative scale of importance. Kundera's metaphor for this purpose is the movable observation tower. The author discusses it with his readers in [*Life Is Elsewhere*].... The observatory is mentioned again in *The Book of Laughter and Forgetting*, along with several closely related images.... In this novel about memory and awareness, background and foreground, past and present, the recollected trivia and forgotten loves are ever shifting and sliding past each other. Russian tanks invade the country, and Mother is thinking about some pears the pharmacist promised her. Shocking. Or is it? In a beautiful image Kundera describes Mother's perspective: A big pear in the foreground and somewhere off in the distance a tank, tiny as a ladybug, ready at any moment to take wing and disappear from sight. So Mother was right after all: tanks are mortal, pears eternal.... (pp. 206-07)

Are tanks more important than pears? Questions, and still more questions. The very structure of *The Book of Laughter and Forgetting* is a question, for, as Kundera explains, the book is not so much a novel as a book of variations and what are variations if not a spiral of questions about a single theme? In a broader sense, Kundera's prose writings as a whole can be seen as variations on a few related themes: awareness and self-deception, the power of human lucidity and its limits, the games of history and love.

Kundera's fiction is a game of wits in which deception is one of the main strategies. Ludvik, the hero of *The Joke*, feigns love for Helena as part of his scheme of revenge. *The Farewell Party* is a comedy of deception, while *The Book of Laughter and Forgetting*, and many of Kundera's short stories are ironic dissertations on the arts of erotic trickery. The distinctive feature of Kundera's fiction, however, is not merely that his characters resort to guile in order to outwit fate and each other; his heroes and heroines also frequently deceive themselves. In fact, self-deception is such a striking element in Kundera's stories and novels that his protagonists could really be divided into two moral types: those who are satisfied to remain self-deluded and those struggling for a measure of self-awareness.

Self-deception is often unmasked when a character is called upon to take action. In Kundera's world a crucial step is frequently taken without clear motivation or deliberation, impulsively, catching the psyche exposed like a sudden, involuntary glimpse of one's face in a mirror. In *The Farewell Party* a book about death and birth, yet Kundera's most playful novel, a pivotal point occurs when the pregnant Ruzena reaches for a pill held in the palm of her adversary Jakub. Ruzena believes the pill to be a tranquilizer, but as Jakub knows perfectly well, it actually contains poison: Jakub stared into her eyes, then slowly, ceremoniously, he opened his hand. For a moment he is vouchsafed a searing flash of insight into the meaning of his behavior.

Raskolnikov experienced his act of murder as a tragedy, and staggered under the weight of his deed. Jakub was amazed to find that his deed was weightless, easy to bear, light as air. And he wondered whether there was not more horror in this lightness than in all the dark agonies and contortions of the Russian hero....

In a masterpiece of concise irony, the narrator describes Jakub's meditation on guilt: The One testing him (the nonexistent God) wished to learn what Jakub was really like and not what he pretended to be like. And Jakub decided to be honest in the face of his examiner, to be the person he really was.... Who, then, is Jakub? The one pretending to be Jakub, or the one who decided to be Jakub? Can someone deciding to be honest at the same time be honest?

One form of self-deception to which Kundera's protagonists are prone may be called bad faith, a moral syndrome reminiscent of the mauvaise foi first diagnosed in the modern consciousness by Jean-Paul Sartre. This bad faith is consciously induced self-deception whereby people pretend to themselves to be unaware of certain realities in order to postpone the need for making decisions. (p. 207)

Mauvaise foi is a philosophical concept, and its applicability to literary characters is only implicit. Yet there are remarkable parallels between Sartre's paradigm and several situations in Kundera's novels. In *Life Is Elsewhere* the artist kisses Maman, and subsequent reflection could not change what had happened but only establish the fact that something wrong had taken place. But Maman could not be sure even of that, and so she postponed solving the problem until some future time.... (pp. 207-08)

Similarly, in *The Book of Laughter and Forgetting*, Tamina perhaps the most attractive and intriguing of Kundera's heroine tries to suppress her awareness of sexual intimacy with Hugo by concentrating on vacations spent with her late husband, a mental effort Kundera compares to an exercise in irregular verbs. But why did Tamina refuse to defend herself? asks the narrator. He (not she Czech grammar is clear about the gender of anonymous narrators) is puzzled, for it is not only the protagonists or readers who struggle for awareness; the narrator too begins in a state of partial ignorance and gains knowledge slowly, painfully, as the story progresses....

Why is self-awareness so difficult to achieve? Kundera does not look to Freud for the answer. People fool themselves because truth is elusive and fragmented, and because they are losing touch with memory and history....

The hero of *The Joke* still had a name and a tradition, was rooted in a specific time and place. Memory, in *The Joke*, has an ambiguous significance: the loss of tradition, as exemplified by the banalization of the ancient "Ride of the Kings," is to be deplored, but forgetfulness is also a necessary means of healing and reconciliation. Nothing will be forgiven, writes Kundera, but everything will be forgotten.

However, by the time the cycle of novels has culminated in *The Book of Laughter and Forgetting*, (and the 1968 invasion of his land has faded from the world's conscience), amnesia has become for Kundera a clear-cut metaphor for individual and national destruction. After *The Joke* Kundera's novels grow more a historical and parodic, with characters designated by first names or occupational categories. *The Farewell Party* takes place in a spa, far from Prague and close to the border of national and geographic anonymity. In *The Book of Laughter and Forgetting* Kundera shifts back and forth from a very real Prague to a painfully recollected homeland and finally to an Atlantis of blissful amnesia, an innocent island suggestive of a miniature America as well as the land of Lilliput.

The discontinuity with the past, the generational amnesia, is reflected in several of Kundera's novels by the search for a missing parent more specifically a missing father, the *pater absconditus*. (p. 208)

From his high-rise tower in Brittany, from his Paris window, Milan Kundera is still looking east toward Prague, toward his Moravian birthplace, toward the Central Europe he considers his spiritual home. What is there in his work that is descended from Czech literary traditions? The novel of ideas has never taken root in Czech culture, nor has the kind of intellectual game Kundera plays with Eros and politics, fiction and reality. Czech readers are more used to laughing than to exploring the sources of laughter, and pure jeu d'esprit has appeared in modern Czech literature only rarely and belatedly.

Kundera's real literary roots are in the eighteenth century, in the digressive storytellers, in Sterne and especially in the French ironists and Encyclopedists. In his recent works, particularly *The Book of Laughter and Forgetting*, as Kundera leaves the land of Bohemia and views the little figures of the world panorama from an ever higher observatory, his irony often changes to Swiftian satire, and to Swiftian pessimism. Among modern writers, he has expressed an affinity for Thomas Mann, for Anatole France, for the existentialists, for the Central European writers with a philosophical bent. As he put it in a 1963 interview: Precision of thought moves me more than precision of observation....

The bulk of Kundera's work has never been published in his homeland, but he does not bewail the necessity of writing for foreigners. He thinks the era of parochial national literatures is over, and he believes in the Goethean concept of a world community of letters. The knowledge that he is dependent on translators has affected Kundera's style, inducing him to make his expression clearer, more decisive, less subject to misinterpretation....

Kundera's purely literary paternity may be European rather than specifically Czech, but he has many qualities which have come to be associated with Czech culture: skepticism, dislike of hubris and gigantism, insistence on a human scale as the ideal measure of values, the use of humor as a means of demystification. Very much in the Czech tradition too is the writer as teacher and moralist.... It is hard to say just what effects Kundera's strong political engagement has on his fiction. There is no doubt that his fervor and the associated lyrical emotions he is at such pains to suppress have added power to his high-energy writing and have given his fiction its unusual interplay of polis, Eros and Thanatos. Of course, there is a price to be paid when ironic detachment and inquisitive attitude are replaced by assertions, particularly when those assertions are questionable. Is the cultural impact of the East really so one-sidedly detrimental? What are the origins of the triviality, amnesia, infantility of the modern world? Or its genocidal propensities? As the genially insane physician of *The Farewell Party* so hilariously and chillingly shows, super rationality is never very far from irrationality.

In interviews and statements Kundera may engage in polemics, but in his novels, stories and plays this great author's most personal voice sounds a dialogue with the truth. After publication of *The Joke*, Czech novelist and playwright Ivan Klima wrote: In his passionate desire to reach the truth, no matter how bitter; to resist every illusion, no matter how modestly formulated; to eradicate all myths, no matter how innocent-looking, Milan Kundera has gone further than anyone in the history of Czech prose. This is still true today. (p. 209)

JOHN BAYLEY

Kundera and Kitsch

There is always comedy in the ways in which we are impressed by a novel.
It can either impress us (if, that is, it is one of the very good ones) with the
sort of truths that Nietzsche, Kafka and Dostoevsky tell us, or with the truths
that Tolstoy and Trollope tell us. To the first kind we respond with
amazement and delight, awe even. 'Of course that's it! Of course that's it!'
The second kind of truths are more sober, more laboriously constructed,
more ultimately reassuring. They are the truths necessary for fiction, and
therefore necessary for life. The first kind contribute brilliantly not to life
itself but to what seems an understanding of it. And that too is necessary for
us, or at least desirable, and enjoyable.

   Milan Kundera's latest novel is certainly one of the very good ones. It
is in fact so amazingly better than anything he has written before that the
reader can hardly believe it, is continually being lost in astonishment. In
manner and technique it is not much different from his previous books, but
the story here at last really compels us, and so do the hero and heroine.
Kundera's great strength has always been his wit and intelligence, and his
particular way with these assets. He was a Nietzschean truth teller rather
than a Tolstoyan one. But this new novel [*The Unbearable Lightness of Being*]
dissolves my distinction while at the same time drawing attention to it. Its

From *London Review of Books*, Vol. 6, No. 10, June 7-20. © 1984 by *London Review of Books*.

impact is considerable. Whether it will last, whether one will want to read it again, are more difficult questions to answer.

Salman Rushdie described *The Book of Laughter and Forgetting*, which appeared in English in 1980, as 'a whirling dance of a book,' and went on to bury it under all the chic epithets, sad, obscene, tender, wickedly funny, wonderfully wise, 'a masterpiece full of angels, terror, ostriches and love.' It was not as bad as that. But Kundera was like a man let loose among all the literary fashions of the West, grabbing this and that, intoxicated by the display patterns of freedom. On the publication of the book the Czech Government revoked his citizenship. Both this decision and the book itself followed logically from Kundera's early novels and stories, like *The Joke*, published in Prague during the Prague Spring. *The Book of Laughter and Forgetting* (the title is shorter in Czech and sounds better) used every device of French and American 'fictiveness,' and its pornography, though cheerful, was so insistent in repudiating any shadow of Iron Curtain puritanism that it now seems as didactic and determined as the evolutions of Komsomol girls in red gymslips.

Unfair maybe, but circumstances made the book weightless, cosmopolitan. Despite its title, there is nothing weightless about *The Unbearable Lightness of Being*. In one sense, indeed, it satirises its predecessor. Nor could it possibly have been written by a Frenchman or an American. It is deeply, centrally European, both German and Slav, as Nietzsche himself was both Pole and German. Prague is the centre of this Europe, and with this book we are right back in Kafka's city, where neither Kafka nor Kundera can be published. None the less, Kundera's intelligence has quietly forsaken contemporary Western fashion and gone back to its deep roots, in Europe's old repressions and nightmares, to a time and an art long before the cinema and the modern happening.

Both in Poland and in Czechoslovakia the cinema represented a method of escape into the modernity which the Communist system rejected and forbade. Kundera was a professor of film technology and his pupils produced the new wave in the Czech cinema. His work, even the present novel, has been influenced by film techniques, but they have here been thoroughly absorbed into the forms of traditional literature, and Kundera now seems positively old-fashioned in the way in which he combines the authorial presence with the 'story.' The author is the purveyor of Nietzschean truth, but the story is of the Tolstoyan kind. Lightness of being is associated with the author's voice, with the cinema and sex, with irresponsibility and definition, with politics. Weight or heaviness of being, on the other hand, is associated with love and fidelity, suffering, chance, fiction, form and content ('The sadness was form, the happiness content. Happiness filled the space of sadness'), death.

The story has weight, though it is lightly told. A Prague surgeon, an insatiable womaniser, visits a hospital in a small provincial town. He gives a kind smile to a waitress at the hotel, who falls in love with him. She follows him to Prague. She has weight (her whole background is described). They make love in order to sleep together afterwards (he has never been able to sleep with a woman before, only to make love to her). They are necessary to each other, but he cannot give up other girls. At night his hair smells of them, though he always remembers carefully to wash the rest of himself, and Tereza in her unbearable jealousy has nightmares, dreams that are part of the lightness of being. He marries her to make up for it.

He gets a good job in Zurich, but his habits continue, and Tereza leaves him, goes back to Prague. Realising he cannot live without her, he goes back too, just in time for the Russian invasion. He loses his job, becomes a window-washer, then a driver on a collective farm. With their dog Karenin, he and Tereza remain together. Fate is a story; fate is Beethoven's Es muss sein. Karenin dies of cancer, a moving episode—for animals, being powerless, have all the weight lacking in human consciousness. We learn that Tomas and Tereza die in a car accident, but the novel goes on, leaving them at a moment of settled happiness not unlike the tranquil ending of a traditional novel, on what is presumably their last night on earth. Tomas might have been a successful surgeon in Zurich; he might have emigrated to America, as one of his weightless mistresses, Sabina, has done, and lived in the permanent limbo of non-fiction. But his destiny is the Tolstoyan story and Tereza, who could never 'learn lightness.'

In one sense, then, Kundera's novel neatly turns the tables on today's theorists about the novel. It is, after all, ironical that we are now told all the time how totally fictive fiction is, while the writers who hold this view do not in practice make much effort to render their novels thoroughly fictive—that is, convincingly real. When the novel begins to insist that it is all made up, it tends to strike the reader as not made up at all. Kundera's aim is to emphasize that the novel is, or was, true to one aspect of human life, while the free play of thought and consciousness is true to another.

What then shall we choose? Weight or lightness?

Parmenides posed this very question in the sixth century before Christ. He saw the world divided into pairs of opposites ...
Which one is positive, weight or lightness?

Parmenides responded: lightness is positive, weight negative.

Was he correct or not? That is the question. The only certainty is: the lightness/weight opposition is the most mysterious, most ambiguous of all.

Kundera thus ingeniously suggests that the aspects of life that constitute a novel about it, a determined story, are as authentic as the sense of consciousness, the lightness of being. To understand either we require both. Tomas stands for lightness, Teresa for weight. This sounds as if they were not 'real' characters: but they are, because of the opposition between them.

It would be senseless for author to try to convince reader that his characters had actually lived. They were not born of a mother's womb; they were born of a stimulating phrase or two or from a basic situation. Tomas was born of the saying 'Einmal ist keinmal.' Tereza was born of the rumbling of a stomach.

Tereza was overcome with shame because her stomach rumbled when Tomas first kissed and possessed her. It was empty from the strain of her traveling and she could do nothing about it. Not being able to do anything about it is the sense in which we live as if we were being controlled by the plot of a novel. Tomas is a personified symbol of the German saying, of the idea that nothing ever happens to us because it can only happen once. Because nothing ever happens we can control it—it becomes as light as feathers, like history. 'Because they deal with something that will not return, the bloody years of the French Revolution have turned into mere words, theories and discussions, frightening no one.' We also read this:

> Not long ago I caught myself experiencing a most incredible sensation.
>
> Leafing through a book on Hitler, I was touched by some of his portraits: they reminded me of my childhood. I grew up during the war; several members of my family perished in Hitler's concentration camps; but what were their deaths compared with the memories of a lost period of my life, a period that would never return?

This reconciliation with Hitler reveals the profound moral perversity of a world that rests essentially on the nonexistence of return, for in this world everything is pardoned in advance and therefore everything cynically permitted.

Well, it doesn't follow. Nietzschean discoveries, however sensational, in practice leave common sense and common morality much as they were.

One such reconciliation with Hitler does not alter the general sense of things, or even that of the man who has made this discovery. Much more important from the point of view of the novel is Kundera's manipulation of two sorts of awareness of things: the light and the heavy, the perpetual and the fictional. It is as if he had decided to write a novel—and perhaps he did—which would acquire its reality by contrasting two theoretical views of how the novel presents it: Virginia Woolf's idea of the perpetual transparent envelope of consciousness, helplessly receiving impressions, and the 'row of gig lamps,' the sequential and determined tale told by a novelist like Arnold Bennett.

The transparent, envelope of promiscuous Tomas is dragged down to earth by the determined—in all senses—weight of the faithful Tereza. He is compelled against his nature to become a character in a novel, the character that she by nature is. Their relation is both funny and moving, dominating the book and giving it the dignity of fiction and its weight. (Kundera reminds us that the rise of the novel is both the expression of ever-increasing self-consciousness, and its antidote. By representing ourselves in fictions we escape from the unbearable insubstantiality of awareness. In Cartesian formula: we create the Archers, therefore we exist.)

Kundera has always been a flashy writer, his chief interest in sexual discussion and gossip. This is of course so common now as to be standard practice, at least for writers in the West, and it always involves a degree of self-indulgence. His flashiness here becomes an asset, however, blending nicely with his fictive strategy, which is to separate the splendid and various experience of sex—the area of lightness and the will, conquest, curiosity and enterprise—from the heavy, fated and involuntary area of love. Love shapes the novel, sex provides the commentary: a facile arrangement, perhaps, but effective. Like Stendhal, Kundera categorises with engaging relish the different sorts of womaniser, notably those whose obsession is lyrical, founded on a romantic ideal which is continually disappointed and, continually reborn, and the epic womaniser, 'whose inability to be disappointed has something scandalous about it. The obsession of the epic womaniser strikes people as lacking in redemption (redemption by disappointment).'

Tomas belongs to the second category. Being a surgeon he could not, with his mistresses, 'ever quite put down the imaginary scalpel. Since he longed to take possession of something deep inside them, he needed to slit them open.' Sabina, Tomas's female counterpart, is similarly questing and capricious. For her love is a kind of kitsch, a breaking of faith and truth, spoiling an honest relationship. As an epic-style female Don Juan she is the ruin of her lover Franz, whose obsession with her is of the lyric variety.

All this schematisation is fairly glib: in his miniature play, *The Stone Guest Pushkin* handles the theme of the light-hearted mistress, and the seducer endlessly fascinated by feminine diversity, with a true depth of art, and it seems likely that Kundera has recalled what Pushkin termed a 'dramatic investigation,' and made it diagrammatic and explicit. More compellingly original is the political aspect of lightness, and the fact that, as Kundera perceives, it forms the normal social atmosphere of a Communist state. No one believes any more in the false weightiness of the ideology of such a state, and since that ideology has replaced old-fashioned and instinctive morality the citizens' personal lives are left in a condition of weightlessness.

Sabina associates the kitsch of love with the overwhelming kitsch of the Communist regime, seeing any long-term personal fidelity or integrity as if it were an analogy of that apotheosis of kitsch, the 'Grand March' towards the gleaming heights of socialism. This Kundera suggests is the vilest outcome of the totalitarian kitsch of our time: that it negates any natural and individual pattern of responsibility and weight in private life. Indeed, in a Communist regime there is no private life, but only bottomless cynicism on the one side and measureless kitsch on the other. Sabina had been trained as a painter in the Socialist Realist manner and she soon learnt to practice a subterfuge which in the end became her own highly original and personal style, and makes her rich and successful when she gets away to the West and then to America. She paints a nicely intelligible socialist reality, but with the aid of a few random drops of red paint, or something of the kind, she conjures up an unintelligible reality beneath it, an evocation of meaningless, and therefore to her saving and liberating, lightness of being. She is filled with repulsion when her admirers in the West mount an exhibition, after she has got out, showing her name and a blurb against a tasteful background of barbed wire and other symbols of oppression conquered by the human spirit. This is the same old kitsch by other means, and Sabina, who has a fastidious taste in such things, protests it is not Communism she is rejecting and getting away from, but kitsch itself. 'Kitsch,' observes Kundera, 'is the aesthetic ideal of all politicians and all political parties and movements ... The brotherhood of man on earth will only be possible on a basis of kitsch.'

It is unfortunately typical of Kundera to run a good idea into the ground, to become increasingly entranced in the development of a lively perception until it spreads too easily. It is thus with kitsch, the concept he opposes to lightness of being, and which he deals with in a lyrical analysis in the penultimate section of the novel. The point of this is that though kitsch opposes itself to lightness of being, the true antithesis to kitsch is the weight of love and death in Tereza, the weight with which she envelops Tomas. Kitsch has no answer to death ('kitsch is a folding screen set up to curtain off death'), just as it has no relation to the true necessities of power and love. Sabina is wholly accurate in her perception of the relation between kitsch and Communism: what she loathes and fears is not Communist 'reality'—persecution, meat queues, overcrowding, everlasting suspicion and shabbiness, all of which is quite honest and tolerable—but Soviet idealism. 'In the world of Communist ideal made real,' the world of Communist films and 'grinning idiots,' 'she would have nothing to say, she would die of horror within a week.'

The term 'kitsch,' as used by Kundera, oversimplifies the whole question of the mechanism by which we accept life and open our arms to its basic situations. All good writers, from Homer to Hemingway, have their own versions of it. If we accept his definition, all art would be as full of kitsch—the stereotyped formula of gracious living—as any Hollywood or Soviet film. What matters, surely, as he also recognises, is the purpose behind kitsch today, the ways in which commercial and political interests have taken over and control a basic human need. Kitsch—the word and its meaning—arrived in the 19th century as a substitute for the other kinds of human illusion, religious and chiliastic, which were withering away. 'What makes a leftist is the kitsch of the Grand March.' Yes, but what makes living endurable is the kitsch of life itself. Here Kundera, it must be said, makes a nice distinction.

> Kitsch causes two tears to flow in quick succession. The first tear says: How nice to see children running on the grass!
> The second tear says: How nice to be moved, together with all mankind, by children running on the grass!
> It is the second tear that makes kitsch kitsch.

Even Sabina comforts herself sometimes with the image of herself as part of 'a happy family living behind two shining windows,' but 'as soon as the kitsch is recognised for the lie it is, it moves into the context of non-kitsch, thus losing its authoritarian power and becoming as touching as any other human weakness.' By always recognising kitsch, Sabina shows herself incapable of those deep involuntary movements of the soul experienced by Tereza, and by Tomas-with-Tereza. Sabina can only know the unbearable lightness of being.

These are old platitudes dressed up in new styles? Inevitably so, to some extent, and like all Nietzschean demonstrators, Kundera cannot afford to admit the relative aspect of things. Kitsch does not define an absolute concept; it only suggests tendency and style. Kundera has a Continental passion for getting things defined, as when he gives us Tereza's dream vision of her death and Tomas's:

> Horror is a shock, a time of utter blindness. Horror lacks every hint of beauty ... Sadness, on the other hand, assumes we are in the know. Tomas and Tereza knew what was awaiting them. The light of horror thus lost its harshness, and the world was bathed in a gentle bluish light that actually beautified it.

In spite of this, his ending is imaginative and very moving, as moving as the end of Kafka's *The Trial*. Indeed Kundera could be said to have written a kind of explication of Kafka's novel, shedding light on its basic allegory and at the same time making use of it for the structure of a new work. Kafka's title is a deep pun. The German word for trial—Prozess—could also refer to the process of living, and it is living which is impossible for Kafka's hero, because all life has been sentenced to death. The strangest moment in *The Trial* is when the hero, about to suffer execution, sees a light go on in a nearby house and someone lean out of the window. That someone is unaware of his fate, or indifferent to it, as the process of living is unaware of death. Kundera the novelist is exceptionally aware, as Kafka was, of the difference between that process and the state of consciousness, of what he calls the unbearable lightness of being. But whereas living for Kafka was not a feasible process, for Kundera it is extremely so. And for him the real enemies of life are not Death and the Law but kitsch and the politician.

MARK STURDIVANT

Milan Kundera's Use of Sexuality

In examining the work of Czechoslavakian author Milan Kundera, critic
Philip Roth observes that "almost all [Kundera's] novels, in fact all the
individual parts of his latest book, find their denouement in great scenes of
coitus" (afterword, *The Book of Laughter and Forgetting*.) Indeed, in Kundera's
most recent effort, *The Book of Laughter and Forgetting*, the novelist follows a
pattern earlier established in his highly acclaimed novel *The Joke* and his
collection of short stories *Laughable Loves* by depicting sexuality as "the focus
where all the themes of the story converge and where its deepest secrets are
located." Kundera views sexuality and eroticism as "the deepest region of
life" and therefore feels that the question of mankind's raison d'circtre, when
"posed to sexuality, is the deepest question." In the expression of this belief
in his three aforementioned [books], sexuality becomes a vehicle for
expressing a variety of interwoven threads of commentary upon human
characteristics, and for ultimately casting a pall of hopelessness and
meaninglessness over mankind's fundamental existence.

Perhaps the most obvious role of sexuality in the portrayal of man
involves the presentation of the characters' innermost concerns and desires,
as sensed by the omniscient narrator, in scenes either during or intimately
related to the sexual act. A clear example of this device, one which explores
what might be termed "the sexual mentality" rather than the act of

From *Critique*, Vol. XXVI, No. 3, Spring, 1985. Copyright © 1985.

intercourse itself, arises in the story "Symposium" in *Laughable Loves*. In accordance with the chief physician's statement that "in eroticism we seek the image of our own significance and importance," Nurse Alzhbeta, a woman with "a hideous face but a beautiful body," protests against what she considers the "sheer absurdity and injustice" of her physical fate by performing a mock striptease. Her frustration and agony increase as a doctor to whom she "brazenly [makes] advances" harshly rejects her, causing her striptease to become increasingly blatant; this progression expresses the character's emotions via a sexually related action....

Perhaps Kundera's most straight-forward presentation of this inability to establish psychological and physical unity occurs in the opening short story of *Laughable Loves*, "The Hitchiking Game." In this story, the young, unnamed female initially believes that her boyfriend "never [separates] her body from her soul" and that "she [can] live with him wholly." However, Kundera suggests the implausibility of such an attitude in a game which the couple choose to play: through changing identities, and fueled by mutual possessive jealousy and relentlessly heightening eroticism, the two characters' thoughts and actions offer another example of the author's viewpoint expressed via sex-dominated circumstances. To her boyfriend, the girl grows more attractive physically as she "[withdraws] from him psychically"; for as he muses that the illusion of her co-existing goodness and beauty which "he worshipped" is "real only within the bounds of fidelity and purity" and that "beyond these bounds she [ceases] to be herself," the young man realizes that "the girl he loved was a creation of his desire, his thoughts, and his faith and that the real girl now standing in front of him [is] hopelessly alien, hopelessly ambiguous." As "the game [merges] with life," the two characters—the girl a prostitute, the boy her client—plunge into frenzied intercourse in which "there [are] soon two bodies in perfect harmony, two sensual bodies, alien to each other." This sexual act causes the girl to acknowledge her irreversible mind/body duality as she, feeling "horror at the thought," realizes that "she [has] never known such pleasure" as that which she experiences beyond the "forbidden boundary" of "love-making without emotion or love."...

Although *The Joke* may carry a more fervent political statement than *Laughable Loves*, the final story of the latter book—"Edward and God"— seems to present the author's thesis on human existence in its most forcefully despairing form. Thus, this second example of the third prong of the author's approach serves as both an ultimate declaration and as an exemplary fusion of the earlier two prongs toward the final destination of Kundera's thesis. In this tale, a lighthearted outlook on sexuality—an approach which might be expected from a book entitled *Laughable Loves*—dominates the beginning of the story as Edward, the protagonist, feigns piety and religious conviction in hopes of establishing sexual relations with the beautiful yet "very reserved and virtuous" Alice. Circumstances favor Edward as party members persecute him for his "religious beliefs," causing Alice in admiration to become "warm, and passionate" and agreeing to prove her affection for Edward by visiting his brother's cottage, "where they could be alone." At this point, the reader, probably awaiting the "Fall of Edward," is not disappointed; however, the use of Edward's long sought sexual encounter with Alice as the actual catalyst for this decline serves to magnify the extent of his misery and to accurately demonstrate the true magnitude of meaninglessness with which Kundera associates the human condition. Edward indeed meets success in his sexual endeavors, yet, as he realizes, "Alice's unexpected turnabout had occurred independently ... of his argumentation ... of any logical consideration whatsoever." Representative of Kundera's belief in the farcical nature of human events, the fulfillment of Edward's consummate desire rests "upon a mistake," and Alice's change of heart had "been deduced quite illogically even from this mistake." Furthermore, representative of Kundera's practice of revealing his characters' most fundamental beliefs in scenes of coitus or some other sexually related situation, Edward is haunted by thoughts of "those long, futile weeks when Alice had tormented him with her coldness" in that Edward now is irritated by "how easily and remorselessly she [is] now betraying her God of No Fornication." Kundera's emphasis on an inescapable mind/body duality, accompanied by an inability to achieve satisfaction in either state, again emerges as Edward realizes that he much favors the "old" Alice, whose "beautiful simplicity of her looks seemed to accord with the unaffected simplicity of her faith, and [whose] simple faith seemed to be a substantiation of her attitude" however, he now "[feels] no joy at all" upon viewing her as "an accidental conjunction of a body, thoughts, and a life's course." Therefore, in an episode marked by demonstration of the fluid and cyclic characteristics of Kundera's overall analysis through sexuality, Edward masters his newly-acquired outlook—using "the words 'disgust' and 'physical aversion'" to attack his lover—by sending Alice home on the train.

The thoughtful reader now may recognize the abnormal (for a Kundera character) degree of control which Edward yields, a characteristic seemingly in direct opposition to the author's attempt to present human existence as farcical, meaningless, and hopelessly uncontrollable. However, Edward's dominance over the course of Alice's departure proves quite misleading: earlier in the story, Edward receives harsh admonitions from the

Communist Party Organization in his town but manages to avoid serious disciplinary action through clever lies, which indicate his self-declared failure to "take them seriously." However, the very depth of knowledge which distinguishes Edward from most Kundera characters creates a new degree of meaninglessness and hopeless relegation to life without control, for not only is his existence plagued by these factors, he realizes and understands that "the shadow that mocks remains a shadow, subordinate, derivative, and wretched, and nothing more." Kundera seems to demand "What else can knowledge accomplish?" as Edward realizes that "what [has] happened, [has] happened, and it [is] no longer possible to right anything."

An ideal conclusion—yet Kundera apparently feels that additional "circumstantial evidence" will better hammer home his thesis. Therefore, after depicting Edward as reasonably content with his routine of sex with the directress of the Communist Party Organization (yes, yet another twist in plot) and of solitary walks, Kundera uses parenthesis to imply direct author-reader contact as he invites the reader to join him in viewing Edward visiting the local church. This final scene in *Laughable Loves*, involving Edward while sitting in the quiet sanctuary suddenly smiling a broad smile in the midst of his sorrow, might be interpreted three ways. However, two of the possible interpretations are apparently refuted by evidence given in context, leaving the third as the plausible, forceful, and rightful conclusive analysis of Kundera's evaluation of human existence. And as in his other works, the author's conclusive statement evolves from thoughts and actions based on sex-related relationships. The first of the possible renditions holds that Edward indeed sees "the genuine living face of God" and thus smiles in rapture. However, Kundera earlier insists that "Edward did not believe in God" and assures the reader that "our story does not intend to be crowned with the effect of so ostentatious a paradox"; these inserts, coupled with another author-to-reader statement in parenthesis describing God as "alone and nonexistent," severely damage the credibility of this first interpretation.

Secondly, upon recalling Kundera's penchant for surprise and his belief in man's inability to clearly judge events affecting his life, the reader might interpret the author's purpose for the final scene as "the last word" concerning Edward's lack of true judgment as he is ultimately deceived into a belief in God. Once again, however, the arguments refuting the first explanation are applicable in this case, and seem to overpower additional opposing suggestions such as the possibility of Kundera's description of God as "nonexistent" being more accurately analyzed as the author's depiction of God as a spirit rather than a member of "this unessential (but so much more existent) world."

This leaves only a third evaluation, a stance supported both by the intricacies of the final scene as well as by the story, and its foundation of use of sexuality, as a whole. This final interpretation holds that Edward, in his tragic awareness, realizes the full magnitude of the hopelessly farcical and meaningless connotations of human existence and crosses The Border [described by Kundera as "a certain imaginary dividing line beyond which things appear senseless and ridiculous"] as he smiles a smile not of "imitation laughter" but of "original (the Devil's)" laughter (*The Book of Laughter and Forgetting*), the laughter of hopeless despair. Supporting this explication of the last page of "Edward and God" and of *Laughable Loves*, the portrayal of Edward as cognizant of man's position continues as he is "too bright to concede that he [sees] the essential in the unessential." But he nonetheless longs "for God ... the essential opposite of this unessential ... world," for he is "too weak not to long secretly" for a means of removing his burden of knowledge and subsequent sorrow, which has developed via his various sexual encounters. Despite this hope, he soon recognizes that which Kundera has earlier told the reader—that God is nonexistent—and the depth of his and mankind's ignominious fate is mirrored in the terrible irony of the narrator describing this revelation as the emergence of "the genuine living face of God." The narrator, whose view now lacks the tone of intimacy earlier described in Kundera's comments in parenthesis, sadly misinterprets Edward's smile as "happy"; a more accurate approach, signified by a sense that Kundera inserts his comments since it does not smoothly follow from the previous statement (Edward as "too weak not to long secretly for the essential"), emerges in the thought that "a man lives a sad life when he cannot take anything or anyone seriously." Kundera needlessly urges the reader to "keep him (Edward) in your memory with this smile."

ROGER KIMBALL

The Ambiguities of Milan Kundera

The Czech novelist Milan Kundera was in his late thirties when he published his first novel, *The Joke*, in Prague in 1967. The book traces the fortunes and amours of a young student, Ludvik, after his exasperatingly patriotic girlfriend decides to show the authorities a postcard he had written her as a joke: Optimism is the opium of the people! A healthy atmosphere stinks of stupidity! Long live Trotsky! Ludvik. As a result of this whimsy, Ludvik finds himself expelled from the Communist Party and the university, and is eventually conscripted to work in the mines for several years.

The appearance of Kundera's acerbically political novel coincided with—indeed, it was only possible in—the short-lived liberalization of Czech society that has come to be known as the Prague Spring. *The Joke* went through three large printings in quick succession and instantly won Kundera a wide and enthusiastic readership in his homeland. It also won him the somewhat less enthusiastic attention of the Communist Party. At the end of August, 1968, Russian troops abruptly occupied Czechoslovakia, putting an end to the Prague Spring and the reformist government of Alexander Dubcek. In a bitterly ironic variation on the fate of his character Ludvik, Kundera was relieved of his teaching position at the Prague Film School and deprived of the right to work. *The Joke* was banned and removed from public

From *The New Criterion*, Vol. IV, No. 5, January, 1986. © 1986 by *The New Criterion*.

libraries—erased, as Kundera put it, from the history of Czech literature. Finally, in 1975, Kundera emigrated to France, where he has since resided.

Kundera first came to the notice of American readers in the mid-Seventies with a collection of short stories, *Laughable Loves* (1974), and *The Farewell Party* (1976), a novel. Together they earned him a small but devoted following among aficionados of contemporary fiction. But it was not until the publication of *The Book of Laughter and Forgetting* in 1980 that Kundera really established himself among the American literary intelligentsia—though, in fact, *The Book of Laughter and Forgetting* did not so much establish Kundera's reputation here as enshrine it; it elevated him to that pantheon of writers whose productions exist more as untouchable objects of admiration than as works susceptible to critical commentary. And Kundera's latest novel, *The Unbearable Lightness of Being* (1984), only confirmed his apotheosis. Most reviewers dispensed with criticism altogether and instead vied with one another to concoct suitably handsome words of praise. Not merely brilliant, daring, or provocative, *The Unbearable Lightness of Being* was widely held to constitute Kundera's patent of literary immortality, establishing him, in the words of one reviewer, as the world's greatest living writer.

Now, Kundera is indisputably a writer of enormous talent. Especially at a time when fiction in this country seems caught somewhere between the dreary banalities of Ann Beattie, the quasi-pornographic imaginings of John Hawkes, and the narcissistic obscurities of Donald Bartholomew, he appears as a novelist of almost preternatural force and inventiveness. But precisely because Kundera has assumed such eminence, his work deserves more than indiscriminate celebration. Though he has developed a voice that is unmistakably his own, his best work exercises an appeal that can be said to epitomize the ethos of contemporary dissident fiction: fiercely intellectual, it is charged with a cool, at times almost brutal eroticism and ironic humor, and it is everywhere at pains to declare its fictionality, to call attention to its novelistic status. Thus in coming to appreciate the distinctive appeal of Kundera's fiction—its substance, its vitality, its challenging idiosyncrasies—we may also come to understand one of the most important (if also perhaps one of the most problematic) aspects of contemporary fiction generally.

At the same time, we may discover something about the sensibility of the audience for this species of contemporary fiction. For despite its obvious literary sophistication, Kundera's work is also deeply political, drawing heavily on his experience of totalitarianism in an effort to explore the difficult spiritual landscape that his characters populate. Kundera has by no means always affirmed his status as a dissident writer; on the contrary, especially in recent years, he has striven to qualify, even deny, that status at every turn. But it is, I believe, in the political dimension of his work—or, more accurately, in the ambiguous attitude Kundera adopts toward the political dimension of his work—that we will find an important source of his tremendous appeal both in this country and in Western Europe.

The identity of a people or civilization, Kundera wrote in an essay that appeared in the English quarterly *Granta*, is always reflected and concentrated in what has been created by the mind—in what is known as 'culture.' Many, perhaps most, of us tend to equate the culture of Czechoslovakia and its Austro-Hungarian neighbors with the culture of Eastern Europe. That we should so blithely cede the cultural as well as the political heritage of these countries no doubt tells us much about the nature and success of the Soviet Union's custodianship there. According to Kundera, though, the defining cultural impulse of that area has its source not in the patrimony of the East but in the spiritual legacy of the West. What does Europe mean to a Hungarian, a Czech, a Pole? he asks. Their nations have always belonged to the part of Europe rooted in Roman Christianity. They have participated in every period of its history. For them, the word 'Europe' does not represent a phenomenon of geography but a spiritual notion synonymous with the word 'West.'

In proclaiming this cultural affiliation with Western Europe, Kundera underscores his allegiance to the fundamental Enlightenment values of skeptical rationality and individualism—traditional liberal values that he summarized in another essay as respect for the individual, for his original thought, and for his inviolable private life. It is no secret that these values have come increasingly under siege in modern society, most brutally and systematically in totalitarian regimes, but also, Kundera would insist, in democratic regimes, where the imperatives of mass culture compromise private life and discount genuine individuality. It is of course this latter insistence—that freedom and man's privacy are threatened as much in Western democracies as under Communism—that has won Kundera so many friends on the Left, for whom the defiant, anti-Communist stance of the dissident writer is perfectly acceptable provided that his defiance extends to all expressions of authority, notably to those that provide a haven for his dissidence. But taken in conjunction with his attempt to downplay the frankly political message of his work, Kundera's criticisms of the West highlight ambiguities at the heart of his position—ambiguities that force us to question the good faith and ideological motives of this troubling writer.

Time and again, Kundera has praised the wisdom of the novel as a counter to the leveling influence of modern society. In the midst of an environment hostile to private life and the integrity of the individual, the novel appears as a sanctuary where the precious essence of European individualism is held safe as in a treasure chest. It is thus not surprising that the major thematic concern of Kundera's fiction, from *The Joke* through *The Unbearable Lightness of Being*, is with the fate of the individual in modern society, especially in modern Communist society.

Of course the fate of the individual in modern society is hardly uncharted territory for novelists. But this venerable theme breathes with new life in Kundera's work, in large part because of the adroit way in which he manages to interweave fact and fiction. His characters occupy a stage that is defined half by Kundera's imagination, half by the historical reality of recent Czech history. He tends to work with extremely short chapters and a shifting, episodic narrative that together create a montage of images, story lines, and characterizations. To this end, he has developed a terse, sinewy style, sharply ironical yet urgently engaged. The narrative is constantly interrupted as Kundera steps back to impart a bit of philosophy, autobiography, or psychological conjecture. *The Unbearable Lightness of Being*, for example, begins with a reflection on Nietzsche's doctrine of the eternal return—a reflection that itself returns to become one of the book's leitmotifs—and *The Book of Laughter and Forgetting* is studded with straightforward factual accounts of historical incidents.

In many ways, *The Book of Laughter and Forgetting* is Kundera's most accomplished work to date. With it he perfected his digressive narrative technique, in which themes are stated, developed, transformed, and interwoven more or less on the model of a musical variation—an analogy that Kundera has been fond of invoking when describing his writing. Yet in *The Book of Laughter and Forgetting*, Kundera's variations—his excursions into philosophy, say, or intellectual history—never strike one as being mere intellectual decorations, inessential to its life as a novel, as they do, at times, in *The Unbearable Lightness of Being*. The book follows the melancholy, often overlapping careers and erotic entanglements of several sets of characters as they struggle to salvage some sense of joy and vitality, some sense of themselves as individuals, against the bleak backdrop of present-day Czechoslovakia. Kundera pauses throughout to descant on subjects as diverse as mass psychology, the nature of the novel, and the fate of various heroes of the Czech resistance. In one of two key chapters entitled "The Angels," for example, Kundera suddenly interrupts his story, recalling that

> [Soon] after the Russians occupied my country in 1968, I (like thousands and thousands of other Czechs) lost the privilege of working. No one was allowed to hire me. At about that time some

young friends started paying me regular visits. They were so young that the Russians did not have them on their lists yet and they could remain in editorial offices, schools, and film studios. These fine young friends, whom I will never betray, suggested I use their names as a cover for writing radio and television scripts, plays, articles, columns, film treatments—anything to earn a living. I accepted a few of their offers, but most I turned down. I couldn't have gotten to them all, for one thing, and then too it was dangerous. Not for me, for them. The secret police wanted to starve us out, cut off all means of support, force us to capitulate and make public confessions. They kept their eyes out for all the pitiful little escape routes we used to avoid encirclement, and they meted out severe punishments to the friends who gave me their names.

Characteristically, this sober report is sandwiched between two very different and seemingly unrelated narratives, the first installment of a tale about two naive American schoolgirls at summer school abroad preparing a presentation on Ionesco's *Rhinoceros*, and Kundera's essayistic elaboration of a metaphysics of laughter. His commitment to irony naturally leads him to extol laughter, but he is careful to distinguish two kinds of laughter: demonic laughter, which is fundamentally dissenting, lonely, even nihilistic, and angelic laughter, which sentimentally rationalizes a world whose contradictions and sufferings it deliberately blinds itself to. It follows that, in Kundera's bestiary, Devils, though essentially a negative, admonitory force, manifest an heroic skepticism that immunizes them to the hypocrisy of sentimentality; Angels, on the other hand, acquiesce in illusion and refuse to acknowledge the lie at the heart of the utopia they crave.

What Kundera calls demonic laughter plays an enormously important role in his work. Though his fiction can be as freighted with existential pathos as anything by Sartre or Camus or Kafka, it is nevertheless possessed of a levity and insouciance that make it as entertaining as it is thoughtful. His depiction of the American schoolgirls' report on *Rhinoceros*, for example, crystallizes the book's central themes in a moment of surreal, demonic hilarity.

Given the self-consciously playful character of Kundera's novels, it is hardly surprising that he cites Sterne's *Tristram Shandy* and Diderot's *Jacques le fataliste* as crucial inspirations. And while the tone and feel of Kundera's fiction is distinctly more modulated—more linear, one might say—than those rambunctious early novels, their influence can be felt throughout his work, both in its self-consciously digressive narratives and in the ironic humor that Kundera insinuates into even his most stringent philosophical meditations.

Closer to hand, Kundera's humor reminds one even more of the great Austrian novelist Robert Musil, whose sprawling, unfinished masterpiece, *The Man without Qualities*, is perhaps the most profound and certainly the funniest portrait of decaying fin-de-siecle Austrian culture we possess. Kundera has not created any character as memorable as Musil's Ulrich—the protagonist of *The Man without Qualities* nor has he rivaled Musil's scope or incisive social satire; but his fiction bristles with a kindred ironic, highly intellectualized wit.

Kundera also specializes in that brand of emotionally distanced, often farcical, eroticism that has become a hallmark of so much modernist and postmodernist fiction. Here again, we can see the influence of the ribald tradition of Sterne and Diderot. Diderot's novel especially is celebrated by Kundera for its explosion of impertinent freedom without self-censorship, of eroticism without sentimental alibis.

In fact, though, Kundera's depictions of sex are edged with a loneliness and even desperation quite absent from the more playful work of his acknowledged precursors. His fiction abounds in explorations of what we might call intimacy in distress. The erotic lives of his characters become a theater in which a wounded individuality, half capitulating to forces inimical to it, struggles to preserve itself. As Kundera put it in the interview with Philip Roth that appears as the afterword to *The Book of Laughter and Forgetting*, "with me everything ends in great erotic scenes. I have the feeling that a scene of physical love generates an extremely sharp light which suddenly reveals the essence of characters and sums up their life situation."

There are dramatic and usually unhappy sexual liaisons throughout Kundera's work, generally centering on his characters' inability to combine love with sexual passion. Physical love only rarely merges with spiritual love, he concludes sadly in *The Joke*. Particularly revealing, I think, are Tomas's reflections on erotic friendship in *The Unbearable Lightness of Being*. They exhibit a thoroughgoing aestheticism that not only typifies Kundera's treatment of erotic matters but also says a good deal about the underlying sensibility of his work tout court.

Like Kierkegaard's aesthete in *Either/Or*, who attempts to defeat boredom by cultivating a systematically arbitrary approach to life, Tomas attempts to establish a compromise between fear and desire by steadfastly avoiding any genuine emotional involvement in his relationships with women. He has become a connoisseur of what Kierkegaard called the rotation method. To insure that erotic friendship never grew into the aggression of love, Kundera explains, Tomas would meet each of his long-term mistresses only at intervals. He considered this method flawless and propagated it among his friends: The important thing is to abide by the rule of threes. Either you see a woman three times in quick succession and then never again, or you maintain relations over the years but make sure that the rendezvous are at least three weeks apart.The rule of threes enabled Tomas to keep intact his liaisons with some women while continuing to engage in short-term affairs with many others. He was not always understood.

The problem for Tomas, as again for Kierkegaard's aesthete, is the intractable reality of his lovers; once they are gone they assume a pleasing poetic existence that can be enjoyed at will without the endless accommodations that any real relationship involves. His love for Tereza was beautiful, but it was also tiring: he constantly had to hide things from her, sham, dissemble, make amends, buck her up, calm her down.... Now [that she had left him] what was tiring had disappeared and only the beauty remained.

There is of course a large element of satire in Kundera's depiction of Tomas, as there is in most of his depictions of intimate feelings. But satire has authority only to the extent that one can discern a credible alternative to the reality being satirized; otherwise it becomes indistinguishable from what it satirizes. And the truth is that Kundera's own aestheticism, his own rebellion against the reality of what he describes, robs his work of any such alternative.

Kundera suggests that erotic intimacy promises a real, if already threatened, refuge for individuality in the modern world; hence he often insists that his books are essentially love stories. Yet it must be said that in Kundera's novels sex is generally a rather chilly, dehumanizing event, an exercise that offers precious little refuge. Not to put too fine a point on it, there is something distinctly creepy about his portrayals of intimate relationships. One thinks, for example, of Ludvik's aborted seductions in *The Joke*, of the amusing but strikingly passionless orgies in *The Book of Laughter and Forgetting*, or of the dismal erotic adventures featured in *Laughable Loves*; in every case what we see is sex in the service of power, betrayal, diversion, or despair, only very rarely in the service of affection or genuine intimacy. Not surprisingly, this aspect of Kundera's work has added greatly to its appeal, especially in the academy, where there is an abiding appetite for this sort of lugubrious depiction of sex.

The cumulative—and carefully calculated effect—of Kundera's style is fiction endowed with a sense of great immediacy and directness, with a nimbus, so to speak, of reality. Though we are everywhere reminded that we are reading fiction, in the end such reminders tend to increase rather than diminish our confidence in the authority and truthfulness of the narrator. It would be senseless for the author to try to convince the reader that his characters once actually lived, Kundera writes of his main characters in *The Unbearable Lightness of Being*. They were not born of a mother's womb; they were born of a stimulating phrase or two or from a basic situation. Tomas was born of the saying 'Einmal ist keinmal' ('Once is never'). Tereza was born of the rumbling of a stomach. It is all merely fiction, yes, but we somehow feel that in admitting this the author is taking us into a deeper confidence, preparing us for some important truth.

By self-consciously warping the border between fact and fiction, Kundera's work manifests a characteristically modernist preoccupation with the relation between art and truth, between art and reality. (pp. 5-10)

[Kundera] would seem to ask whether the beautiful illusions that art produces are to be taken seriously; certainly, his fiction adopts a posture of questioning their apparent self-sufficiency. He continually intrudes images of all that is problematic, insecure, unharmonious about daily life into the untroubled kingdom within which art reigns supreme. But unlike Mann, Kundera does not use the conventions of art to question our faith in art's illusions; rather, he skillfully imports gestures of reality in order to give his fiction an aura of truth and critical weightiness.

Probably the central critical element in Kundera's work is his attack on sentimentality. This takes various forms, and is evident throughout his writing, in his essays as well as his novels. Everywhere there is a deep suspicion of sentimentality, of feeling unscrutinized by doubt. Thus he pokes fun at the obscure depths, the noisy and empty sentimentality of the 'Slavic Soul.' And in his introduction to *Jacques and His Master*, he criticizes Dostoevsky's novels for creating a climate ... where feelings are promoted to the rank of value and of truth.

For Kundera, the battle against sentimentality is at the same time a battle against forgetting. The struggle of man against power, we read at the beginning of *The Book of Laughter and Forgetting*, is the struggle of memory against forgetting. In Kundera's terms, the struggle of memory against forgetting is man's struggle against whatever social or psychological forces would deny the continuity and individuality of his personal history. Hence the attack on sentimentality is only the other side of his defense of individualism. For it is just this—the lonely and irreducible privateness of experience—that sentimentality promises to dissolve. The essential appeal of the sentimental is precisely that it relieves one of the burden of individuality and the responsibilities of adult experience. As the literary critic Northrop Frye observed, sentimentality resists, as a child would do, the inexorable advance of all experience in time, which it tries to arrest by nostalgia....

Sentimentality is the subjective equivalent of the mob's stock response to mood.

It is a version of sentimentality that Kundera explores in *The Book of Laughter and Forgetting* under the name of circle dancing. Circle dancing is his metaphor for the intoxicating lure of the group, the mob, what Frye calls the stock response. Kundera pictures his characters joining together to make a circle. They take two steps in place, one step forward, lift first one leg and then the other.... I think I understand them. They feel that the circle they describe on the ground is a magic circle binding them into a ring. Their hearts are overflowing with an intense feeling of innocence.... Circle dancing is magic. This magic is the spell cast by the dream of a paradise where distinctions vanish and all men are brothers. In this sense paradise tokens not the fulfillment but the denial of the human condition. The longing for Paradise, as Kundera put it, is man's longing not to be man.

Underscoring the political dimension of circle dancing, Kundera confesses that in 1948, after the Communists had taken power in Czechoslovakia, he also danced in a ring, until he was expelled from the Party and had to leave the circle. It was then, he tells us, that he became aware of the magic qualities of the circle, a magic that gives weight to his claim that totalitarianism is not only hell, but also the dream of paradise. (pp. 10-11)

What Kundera dramatizes as circle dancing in *The Book of Laughter and Forgetting* he analyzes as kitsch in *The Unbearable Lightness of Being* and in several occasional essays. While he points out that the term has its origin in Munich art circles in the nineteenth century, for Kundera kitsch refers not simply to a species of bad art but to the deliberate sentimentalization of reality. As Kundera notes, his discussion of kitsch is deeply indebted to the writings of the German novelist and essayist Hermann Broch. Following Broch, he views kitsch not so much as an aesthetic as an ethical or metaphysical category. What we generally think of as kitsch art is for Kundera merely one, rather minor, product of kitsch. Like circle dancing, kitsch is an instrument of forgetting. It offers man an escape from the burden of individuality. Kitsch, he wrote in one essay, is the translation of the stupidity of received ideas into the language of beauty and feeling. In *The Unbearable Lightness of Being*, he remarks that kitsch has its source in the categorical agreement with being, meaning that kitsch involves what he would call an angelic blindness to everything problematic and unaccommodating about experience. Ultimately, the ambition of kitsch is to set up a folding screen to curtain off death.

For Kundera, as for Broch before him, kitsch appears as a universal human temptation. No matter how we scorn it, he writes, kitsch is an integral part of the human condition. In this sense, kitsch bears witness to man's desire to secure himself against the incursions of a reality that can never be adequately mastered. The problem with Kundera's analysis, however, is that by so expanding the meaning of kitsch, he threatens to empty it of critical content. It may be that kitsch cannot be understood as a purely aesthetic category; the aura of moral disapproval that it carries with it suggests that this is the case. But what does it mean, for example, when Kundera asserts that we can regard the gulag as a septic tank used by totalitarian kitsch to dispose of its refuse? There is no doubt that totalitarianism can make effective use of kitsch; but to speak of totalitarian kitsch is to trivialize totalitarianism by assimilating it to a category that has its home in aesthetics; it is in effect to poeticize totalitarianism.

To say, with Kundera, that kitsch is the aesthetic ideal of all politicians and all political parties and movements is to elide just those differences among political parties and movements that really matter. Similarly, when he has a character in *The Unbearable Lightness of Being* compare the sentimental response of an American senator watching children playing on the grass to the smile Communist statesmen beamed from the height of their reviewing stand to the identically smiling citizens in the parade below, he ignores the fact that what matters here is not so much the kitschy sentiment as the uses to which it is put.

The great appeal—and great danger—of concepts like kitsch is that they invite one to discount the real differences among things in the name of a putatively deeper, more essential unity—a unity, however, that enjoys merely a conceptual existence. They thus allow one to maintain a pose of critical distance without the inconvenience of having to make the hard choices that genuine criticism involves. And while there is no doubt that Kundera brings considerable insight—not to mention cleverness—to his explorations of sentimentality, circle dancing, and kitsch, he also indulges in a lamentable tendency to aestheticize these concepts, to use them to disarm the very distinctions they were meant to illuminate.

Kundera's response to this objection would be simply that, as a novelist, he is not in the business of taking positions. Now, not only is the novelist nobody's spokesman, as he put it in one essay, but I would go so far as to say he is not even the spokesman for his own ideas. He goes so far, in fact, as to insist that we view his work as little more than an ironic game, as writing on the level of hypothesis. This is evident, for example, in his objection to being regarded as a political writer. Admitting that he detests Communist regimes, he hastens to add that I detest them as a citizen: as a writer I don't say what I say in order to denounce a regime. A political reading of his work, he suggested in one interview, is a bad reading. Even the label dissident writer annoys him because it imports a political terminology that he claims to be allergic to. Again, in the 1982 preface that he contributed to *The Joke*, Kundera recalled that When in 1980, during a television panel discussion devoted to my works, someone called *The Joke* 'a major indictment of Stalinism,' I was quick to interject, 'Spare me your Stalinism, please. *The Joke* is a love story'—this in a book whose entire psychology is unintelligible without the assumption of such an indictment.

Of course, there is an important sense in which Kundera is right: fiction does exist on the level of hypothesis, not on the level of fact; novels are not position papers. But there is something deeply disingenuous about appeals to the hypothetical or game like character of fiction when those appeals are meant to mask or deny the very real political content of one's work. And this, unfortunately, is the effect of Kundera's rhetoric. For like so many dissident writers, Kundera, though he embraces Western culture and Western freedom, maintains a fundamentally equivocal attitude toward the West. True, as he would be the first to point out, there is much to bemoan about the aggressive superficiality of Western mass culture and the tasteless intrusions of the media into our private lives. But it is one thing to criticize these cultural failings, quite another to pretend that they are in any relevant sense cognate with the evil of totalitarianism—to pretend, that is, that they are somehow merely different versions of the same spiritual malaise.

In fact, though, in statement after statement this is precisely the posture that Kundera has adopted. In an interview with Philip Roth that appeared in *The Village Voice*, for example, Kundera was asked if he thought private or intimate life were less threatened in the West than under Communism. The evolution of the modern world is hostile to intimate life everywhere, he replied. Indeed,

> [in] countries with Communist regimes there's an advantage: we can see clearly what's bad and what's good—if the police tape your private talks, everybody knows that's bad. But in Italy when a photographer lurks around to photograph the face of the mother of a murdered child or the agony of a drowning man, we don't call this a violation of intimacy but freedom of the press.

The implication is clearly that one's privacy and intimate life are just as much in jeopardy in a Western democracy as they are under Communism—

perhaps more insidiously in jeopardy in a democracy, for in a Communist society one at least knows where one stands and there is no attempt to glorify shallow curiosity in the name of freedom of the press. No matter that one's writing, one's livelihood, one's very life are at stake in one society where in another one is coddled and showered with acclaim—essentially the societies must be made to seem two sides of the same coin. Such a pretense is possible only if one substitutes a thoroughly intellectualized—perhaps one should say kitschified—view of the world for the sharper, if less Romantic, discriminations of lived experience. The habits of the media in the West often border on obscenity; but to suggest that the intrusiveness of an Italian news photographer is somehow comparable with the brutality of totalitarianism is absurd. The former may consign one to the front page of a noxious tabloid; the latter abandons one to the cellars of the secret police.

In effect, Kundera wants to have it both ways: he wants both the freedom of fiction and the authority of historical fact; he wants, that is, the cachet of being a dissident writer without the uncomfortably definite political commitments that that status brings with it. Instead, he strives to maintain a completely ironical view of the world, a view that would exempt him from any definite commitment—a view that Friedrich Schlegel, the great theorist of Romantic irony, aptly dubbed transcendental buffoonery. Thus Kundera describes the basic event of *The Book of Laughter and Forgetting* as the story of totalitarianism, which deprives people of memory and thus retools them into a nation of children, and yet still insists that no novel worthy of the name takes the world seriously. But how can a novel recount the story of totalitarianism and not take the world seriously? No one would suggest that Kundera's writing should be reduced to its political content; but to dismiss that content as part of a game, as incidental embellishment or atmosphere to what is really a love story, merely a novel, is to ignore the element that, more than any other, grants it its authority and weight.

Near the end of his essay *Writing*, W. H. Auden remarked that In so far as poetry, or any other of the arts, can be said to have an ulterior purpose, it is, by telling the truth, to disenchant and disintoxicate. In a way, Kundera would seem to agree with Auden's deeply anti-Romantic sentiment. Thus he extols the novel as an ally of individuality—this is its point, its ulterior purpose: to salvage some remnant of individuality in an age when it is threatened by the equalizing pressures of mass media, sentimentality, and totalitarianism. Like Auden, Kundera champions art as a refuge of the critical, ironic, questioning spirit, as a bulwark against the illusions and intoxicating certainties of kitsch, the forgetfulness of circle dancing.

Yet in the end the ambiguities of Kundera's position tend to cut the other way. For by insisting on the purely novelistic status of his work—by denying that a large measure of its authority comes precisely from its seriousness and accurate reflection of social and psychological realities—Kundera brews an intoxicating potion of his own. Indeed, it is all the more powerful for the whiff, the suggestion of truth and reality that it purveys. In this context, we should remind ourselves that criticisms of kitsch, too, can have their kitschy appeal. And it is here, perhaps, that we can witness most clearly the essential ambiguities of Milan Kundera—ambiguities that are not, alas, the inexhaustible ambiguities of human nature but the meaner, more predictable ambiguities of a writer struggling to maintain a predefined image of himself as ideologically correct. (pp. 11-13)

TERRY EAGLETON

Estrangement and Irony

Milan Kundera tells the story in *The Book of Laughter and Forgetting* of a Czech being sick in the middle of Prague, not long after the Soviet invasion of the country. Another Czech wanders up to him, shakes his head and says:

"I know exactly what you mean."

The joke here, of course, is that the second Czech reads as significant what is in fact just a random event. In the post-capitalist bureaucracies, even vomiting is made to assume some kind of instant symbolic meaning. Nothing in Eastern Europe can happen by accident. The logical extreme of this attitude is paranoia, a condition in which reality becomes so pervasively, oppressively meaningful that its slightest fragments operate as minatory signs in some utterly coherent text. Once the political state extends its empire over the whole of civil society, social reality becomes so densely systematized and rigorously coded that one is always being caught out in a kind of pathological 'over reading,' a compulsive semiosis which eradicates all contingency. "No symbol where none intended," Samuel Beckett once remarked; but in 'totalitarian' societies, monolithic structures of meaning, one can never be quite certain what's intended and what isn't—whether there is ominous meaning or not in the delayed arrival of your spouse, the boss's

From *Salmagundi*, No. 73, Winter, 1987. © 1987 by *Salmagundi*.

failure to say good morning, that car which has been behind your own for the past ten miles. Tereza in *The Unbearable Lightness of Being* makes love with an engineer in his flat, but later she will wonder about the drabness of the place compared to his elegance, that edition of Sophocles on the shelf, the few moments he was away making the coffee. Is it the abandoned apartment of an imprisoned intellectual? Is the engineer a police agent, and was he turning on the ciné camera while supposedly making the coffee?

Survival in Eastern Europe demands an awareness of this possible sub-text, a daily hermeneutics of suspicion; but then how, in behaving with such vigilance, is one to avoid becoming collusive with a power for which no event can be accidental, no gesture innocent? How to read without over reading, avoid a naive empiricism without falling prey to semiological paranoia? The most celebrated of all modern Czech writers, Franz Kafka, suspends his readers between narrative and sub-text, the bald appearance of events and the ceaselessly elusive truth of which they might just be dimly allegorical. Such truth is never totalisable, shifting its ground each time one approaches it; there is, perhaps, a metanarrative which rigorously determines the slightest detail of quotidian life but which is always elsewhere. If this is an allegory of the disappeared God, it is also one of the post-capitalist state, a paradoxical condition in which everything is at once compulsively legible, locking smoothly into some univocal story, and yet where history is awash with secrets, whispered treacheries, tell-tale traces. In this drably positivist world, everything lies on the one hand drearily open to view, tediously repetitive and flatly two-dimensional, the mysterious depths of subjectivity drained off from a world which becomes brutely self-identical. On the other hand, nothing is ever quite what it seems; so that a 'postmodernist' eradication of depth, mystery, subjectivity co-exists strangely with a persistent 'modernist' impulse to decipher and decode, a sense of concealment and duplicity.

Kundera's fiction opposes to the sealed-off metanarrative of post-capitalist bureaucracy a set of notably dislocated texts, although not at all in the manner of some sophisticated Western deconstruction. The structural subversiveness of his novels lies simply in the loose capaciousness whereby they encompass different stories, sometimes to the point of appearing like a set of novellas within the same covers. This is not the modernist undermining of narrative realism of a Beckett, for whom one arbitrary story generates another equally gratuitous and then another, until the whole text becomes no more than a machine for pumping out tall groundless tales in an honorable Irish tradition. Each of Kundera's stories has a 'sense' to it, and interacts with the others; but it must be allowed to exist in its own narrative space free from metanarrational closure, absolved from the authoritarianism of the 'closed book.'

Kundera constantly interrupts himself in order to give the slip to the totalitarian drive of literary fiction, breaking off the narrative to deliver his latest ontological musings, inserting a sheaf of brief philosophical reflections between episodes, airily abandoning the fictional pretence in the interests of historical documentation. All of this is done casually, apparently spontaneously, without modernist outrage or obtrusiveness, utterly bereft of any intense aesthetic self-consciousness or portentous experimentalism. There is no sense of shock or rupture in his texts, no heavily calculated violations of plausibility or deftly engineered incongruities, no calculated cacophony of discourses. For this to happen would suggest that one was still in thrall to some literary orthodoxy one was grimly or scandalously intent on discrediting, whereas Kundera conveys the rather more shocking sense of unconcern, a writer who has, so to speak, just not been told that you shouldn't hold up the narrative with metaphysical speculations about angels and devils, and who would not understand what you were talking about if you were to tell him so. He treats the novel as a place where you can write anything you like, anything, as it were, that has just come into your head, as a genre released from constraint rather in the manner of a diary. No doubt, psychobiographically speaking, this artlessness is the effect of a finely conscious art, but his writing bears none of its traces and communicates instead a quite astonishing 'naturalness,' a stunning off-handedness and laid-back companionability which forces the reader genuinely to doubt whether it is in the least aware of its own brilliance. Nothing could be more suspect for the avant-garde West than this spurious naturalisation of the sign, this cavalier lucidity and apparently effortless transparency, which could only for us be yet another craftily contrived style, a cultural sign every bit as eloquent and flamboyant as the laboriously constructed 'degree zero' writing of a Camus or a Hemingway. But our own suspicion of the natural springs from the conditions of a late bourgeois society in which ideology has had several centuries to disseminate itself into the textures of lived experience, crystallizing its devious impulses as the self-evident or commonsensical; in this sense we suspect the 'natural' exactly because ideology has succeeded in its historic task, requiring a violent demystification in fictions which ironise their every proposition. This is not the situation in Eastern Europe, whose political hegemony was only recently installed, moreover, from the outside, and which has therefore had little time or opportunity to flesh itself into a full-blooded phenomenology of everyday life. In such societies, given the

grotesque discrepancy between material hardship and the idealizing claims of
the state, it is ideology which is transparently fictional, portentously self-
conscious, the very reverse of spontaneous or self-evident; and the
'naturalness' of the Kundera style, its easy, intimate relation with the
experiential, is thus as politically significant as is its conversion of the novel
into a space of free-floating discourses in a rigorously codified society.
Kundera's relaxed, unfussy lucidity is post-modernist in a genuine sense of
the word, an art which becomes possible only when all the heart-burnings
and agonisings of modernism proper, its heady transgressions and self-
important experiments, can now at last be taken for granted, put quietly to
use once shorn of their portentousness. For it is exactly that portentousness
which links them, in sensibility if not in doctrine, with the histrionic
posturings of the ideological.

"The only thing we can do," comments one of Kundera's characters
about the writing of fiction, "is to give an account of our own selves.
Anything else is an abuse of power. Anything else is a lie." The paradox of
such liberalism for Kundera is that it keels over inexorably into a kind of
totalitarianism. The narrative of just one individual becomes a closed book,
a sealed, autonomous world every bit as absolute and author-itarian as the
absolutist state. Such solipsism is the mere flipside of Stalinism, sucking
reality into its own self-regulating logic with all the imperiousness of the
central committee. Difference and uniqueness are no salvation in themselves
from the dreary self-identity of the post-capitalist state; the unique has an
unbearable lightness and frailty about it, as though anything which happens
only once might as well not have happened at all. *Einmal ist keinmal*. If
history can be dissolved into pure difference, then the result is a massive
haemorrhage of meaning; because past events only happen once they fail to
take firm root and can be expunged from memory, having about them the
ineradicable aura of pure accident. The past thus perpetually threatens to
dissolve beneath the heel of the present, and this plays straight into the hands
of the absolutist state, devoted as it is to airbrushing disgraced politicians out
of ceremonial photographs. What imbues persons and events with unique
value, then, is precisely what renders them insubstantial, and Kundera's
writing is deeply gripped by this sickening ontological precariousness. Pure
difference cannot be valuable, for value is a relational term; but repetition is
an enemy of value too, because the more something is repeated the more its
meaning tends to fade. Kundera's fiction, both formally and thematically, is
given over to examining this contradiction: it must keep different stories
structurally separate, exploring the distinctiveness of particular relationships

and identities, but always with a profoundly ironic sense of what they share in common, a suspicion that they are in some covert way variations upon a single theme.

The point where difference and identity undecidably converge for Kundera is above all sexuality, linking as it does the unrepeatable quality of a particular love-relationship with the ceaselessly repetitive, tediously predictable character of the bodily drives. What might be thought to be most deviant, stimulating, shockingly unconventional—a sexual orgy—turns out to be hilariously comic in its endless mechanical repetitions, the supposed singularity of erotic love uproariously repeated in a wilderness of mirrors, each individuated body mockingly mimicking the next. Kundera recognizes the profound comedy of repetition, which is one reason why sex is usually the funniest part of his novels: his laughter is that release of libidinal energy which comes from momentarily decathecting the utterly self-identical love-object, the magnificent non-pareil, in the moment of wry recognition that we all share a common biology. The traditional name of this moment is, of course, the carnivalesque, that aggressive onslaught on the fetishism of difference which ruthlessly, liberatingly reduces back all such metaphysical singularity to the solidarities of the flesh. *The Farewell Party* in particular centres upon fertility, child-bearing, procreation, and like several of Kundera's texts is particularly interested in animals.

The political problem of all this is apparent: how is one to use the fleshly solidarity of the human species as a powerfully demystifying force while avoiding that brutal erasure of differences which is Stalinist uniformity? Kundera's anti-Stalinism is interesting precisely because it refuses to fall back upon an unquestioning romantic idealism of the individual; indeed its carnivalesque impulse presses any such romantic idealism to the point of absurdity. The problem is how to stay faithful to that recognition without lapsing into biologistic cynicism, or, as Kundera might himself put it, crossing over that hairthin border which distinguishes 'angelic' meaning from the demonic cackle of meaninglessness. Reproduction, in every sense of the word, may be a source of emancipatory humor, which is one thing Marx meant by suggesting that all tragic events repeated themselves as farce; but the farce in question is destructive as well as redemptive, which was another of Marx's meanings. The bureaucratic state is itself a contradictory amalgam of romantic idealism and cynical materialism: its discourse is the undiluted kitsch of high-sounding sentiment, whereas its practice renders individual bodies and events indifferently exchangeable. It is difficult, then, to subvert its romantic idealism without lapsing into a version of its own lethal leveling. The image of ungainly naked bodies crowded into a single space stirs Kundera to debunking laughter, but it is also for him the image of the concentration camp.

Every time something is repeated, it loses part of its meaning; the unique, however, is a romantic illusion. This is the contradiction within which Kundera struggles, which can be rephrased as an unrelaxable tension between too much meaning and too little. An order in which everything is oppressively meaningful buckles under its own weight: this is the realm of what Kundera names the 'angelic,' which the demonic exists to puncture. The demonic is the laughter which arises from things being suddenly deprived of their familiar meanings, a kind of estrangement effect akin to Heidegger's broken hammer, and which a monstrous proliferation of the supposedly singular can bring about. Meaninglessness can be a blessed moment of release, a lost innocent domain for which we are all nostalgic, a temporary respite from the world's tyrannical legibility in which we slip into the abyss of silence. The demonic is thus closely associated in Kundera's fiction with the death drive, a spasm of deconstructive mockery which, like carnival, is never far from the cemetery. It is a dangerous force, by no means to be euphorically, unqualifiedly celebrated as in the naiveties of some Western deconstruction: it has a malicious, implacable violence about it, the pure negativity of a Satanic cynicism. It is therefore, as Kundera well sees, a tempting lure for the opponents of angelic-authoritarian order, who will be led by it to their doom. The savage irony of the demonic is that it finally dismantles the antithesis of the angels only to conflate the whole of reality indifferently together in a leveling not far from the angels' own. Bodies are interchangeable for both Stalinism and carnival, transgression prized by both revolutionary and cynic. Just as we are precariously positioned by our very bodiliness on an indeterminate frontier between sameness and difference, biology and history, so we must seek to situate ourselves on some almost invisible border between meaning and meaninglessness, embracing all that the angels reject ('shit' is the blunt term Kundera gives to the angelically unacceptable) without settling for that shit like amorphousness which is Stalinism or nihilism. Happiness is the yearning for repetition, but repetition is what erodes it; the male sexual drive, rather like the authoritarian state, is cripplingly divided between a romantic idealism of the particular (the wife, the permanent mistress) and a promiscuous exchangeability of bodies. The novel records these truths, but is itself an image of them: to write is to cross a border where one's own ego ends, creating characters who are neither imaginary self identifications nor opaquely alien, but who repeat the self with a difference.

The novel has its inward necessity, its specific structural logic, but it is also a place where the contingency of existence, the unbearable lightness of being, can be reinvented and to some degree redeemed. When Beethoven, as Kundera reminds us, based a quartet on the words Es muss sein, he weaved an idea of destiny out of what had in fact been a casual joke between himself and a friend. Metaphysical truth was born of playfulness; as in Kundera's *The Joke* a whole metaphysical politics is set in motion by a piece of wit. Human beings, unable to tolerate the frail contingency of their being, must for Kundera rewrite their chance histories as necessity; and this, precisely, is what the novel itself continually does, endowing the accidental with a determinate form. But it is also the characteristic strategy of Stalinism, for which nothing is allowed to escape into pure randomness; and Kundera must therefore write lightly as well as lucidly, bathing what is in the aura of what might not have been. It is for this reason, perhaps, that his narratives are as spare and uncluttered as they are, eschewing the ponderousness of the metaphysical. His cavalier way with them reminds us of their frailness as fictional inventions; and when he speaks in his own voice, the philosophical wisdom he communicates is more the auratic, Benjaminesque 'experience' of the traditional tale-teller than the speculations of a theoretically-minded modernist. What intensities there are in Kundera's work belong, as it were, to the subject-matter rather than to the mode of conveying it, hedged round continually with an irony which represents the borderline between too much meaning and too little, the portentous solemnity of the ideological and the bland dissociation of the cynic.

The dissonance in Kundera between a conventionally romantic subject-matter and a decidedly non-romantic handling of it has itself a political root. For if on the one hand his astonishingly subtle explorations of personal relationships redeems that which Stalinism expels, the ironic pathos with which such relationships are invested is just the reverse of that triumphalistic sentimentality which is Stalinism's ideological stock-in-trade. 'Kitsch' is the name Kundera gives to all such 'shitless' discourse, all such idealizing disavowal of the unacceptable; and in the realm of kitsch, the dictatorship of the heart reigns supreme. Totalitarian kitsch is that discourse which banishes all doubt and irony, but it is not a grim-faced, life-denying speech: on the contrary, it is all smiles and cheers, beaming and euphoric, marching merrily onwards to the future shouting 'Long live life!' The Gulag, as Kundera comments, is the septic tank used by kitsch to dispose of its refuse. If Stalinism cannot be opposed by romanticism it is precisely because it has a monopoly of it; and this is one reason why Kundera's own critique is bent inevitably towards the materialism of the body, whose joyous affirmations must always be radically double-edged, which knows shit and ecstasy together. Carnival generates a collective imagery which can undermine ideological kitsch; but in the end Kundera is unable to accept this, precisely because he comes to define kitsch as any collective imagery whatsoever. His critique of oppressive ideologies is at root curiously formalistic: what seems wrong with kitsch is finally not this or that enunciation or emotion, but the bare fact that it must be a commonly shareable discourse. This is not simply individualist dissent, of a familiarly Eastern European kind: it is that Kundera seems genuinely unable to imagine any universally shared emotion which would not, by definition, be intolerably banal. It is this which leads him to write that "The brotherhood of man on earth will be possible only on a base of kitsch." The best response to this is not to produce the kinds of political argument with which Kundera is doubtless all too familiar; it is simply to point out that any such formulation is untrue to the power of his own fiction. For it is exactly from the irresolvable conflict between the unique and the necessarily repeatable, the fragility of the particular and the comedy of the collective, that his fiction draws part of its formidable strength. To collapse that tension on either side is the real banality; and if Kundera's writing is valuable, it is among other reasons because he makes any such erasure of conflict harder to effect.

ITALO CALVINO

On Kundera

When he was twelve, she suddenly found herself alone, abandoned by Franz's father. The boy suspected something serious had happened, but his mother muted the drama with mild, insipid words so as not to upset him. The day his father left, Franz and his mother went into town together, and as they left home Franz noticed that she was wearing a different shoe on each foot. He was in a quandary: he wanted to point out her mistake, but was afraid he would hurt her. So during the two hours they spent walking through the city together he kept his eyes fixed on her feet. It was then that he had his first inkling of what it means to suffer.

This passage from *The Unbearable Lightness of Being* illustrates well Milan Kundera's art of storytelling—its concreteness, its finesse—and brings us closer to understanding the secret due to which, in his last novel, the pleasure of reading is continuously rekindled. Among so many writers of novels, Kundera is a true novelist in the sense that the characters' stories are his first interest: private stories, stories, above all, of couples, in their singularity and unpredictability. His manner of storytelling progresses by successive waves (most of the action develops within the first thirty pages; the conclusion is already announced halfway through; every story is completed and illuminated layer by layer) and by means of digressions and remarks that transform the private problem into a universal problem and, thereby, one

From *Review of Contemporary Fiction*, Vol. 9, No. 2, Summer, 1989. © 1989 by *Review of Contemporary Fiction*.

that is ours. But this overall development, rather than increasing the seriousness of the situation, functions as an ironic filter lightening its pathos. Among Kundera's readers, there will be those taken more with the goings-on and those (I, for example) more with the digressions. But even these become the tale. Like his eighteenth-century masters Sterne and Diderot, Kundera makes of his extemporaneous reflections almost a diary of his thoughts and moods.

The universal-existential problematic also involves that which, given that we are dealing with Czechoslovakia, cannot be forgotten even for a minute: that ensemble of shame and folly that once was called history and that now can only be called the cursed misfortune of being born in one country rather than another. But Kundera, making of this not "the problem" but merely one more complication of life's inconveniences, eliminates that dutiful, distancing respect that every literature of the oppressed rouses within us, the undeserving privileged, thereby involving us in the daily despair of Communist regimes much more than if he were to appeal to pathos.

The nucleus of the book resides in a truth as simple as it is ineludible: It is impossible to act according to experience because every situation we face is unique and presents itself to us for the first time. "Any schoolboy can do experiments in the physics laboratory to test various scientific hypotheses. But man, because he has only one life to live, cannot conduct experiments to test whether to follow his passion (compassion) or not."

Kundera links this fundamental axiom with corollaries not as solid: the lightness of living for him resides in the fact that things only happen once, fleetingly, and it is therefore as if they had not happened. Weight, instead, is to be found in the "eternal recurrence" hypothesized by Nietzsche: every fact becomes dreadful if we know that it will repeat itself infinitely. But (I would object) if the "eternal recurrence"—the possible meaning of which has never been agreed upon—is the return of the same, a unique and unrepeatable life is precisely equal to a life infinitely repeated: every act is irrevocable, non-modifiable for eternity. If the "eternal recurrence" is, instead, a repetition of rhythms, patterns, structures, hieroglyphics of fate that leave room for infinite little variants in detail, then one could consider the possible as an ensemble of statistical fluctuations in which every event would not exclude better or worse alternatives and the finality of every gesture would end up lightened.

Lightness of living, for Kundera, is that which is opposed to irrevocability, to exclusive univocity: as much in love (the Prague doctor Tomas likes to practice only "erotic friendships" avoiding passionate involvements and conjugal cohabitation) as in politics (this is not explicitly said, but the tongue hits where the tooth hurts, and the tooth is, naturally, the impossibility of Eastern Europe's changing—or at least alleviating—a destiny it never dreamed of choosing).

But Tomas ends up taking in and marrying Tereza, a waitress in a country restaurant, out of "compassion." Not just that: after the Russian invasion of '68, Tomas succeeds in escaping from Prague and emigrating to Switzerland with Tereza who, after a few months, is overcome by a nostalgia that manifests itself as a vertigo of weakness over the weakness of her country without hope, and she returns. Here it is then that Tomas, who would have every reason, ideal and practical, to remain in Zurich, also decides to return to Prague, despite an awareness that he is entrapping himself, and to face persecutions and humiliations (he will no longer be able to practice medicine and will end up a window washer).

Why does he do it? Because, despite his professing the ideal of the lightness of living, and despite the practical example of his relationship with his friend, the painter Sabina, he has always suspected that truth lies in the opposing idea, in weight, in necessity. "Es muss sein!" / "It must be" says the last movement of Beethoven's last quartet. And Tereza, love nourished by compassion, love not chosen but imposed by fate, assumes in his eyes the meaning of this burden of the ineluctable, of the "Es muss sein!"

We come to know a little later (and here is how the digressions form almost a parallel novel) that the pretext that led Beethoven to write "Es muss sein!" was in no way sublime, but a banal story of loaned money to be repaid, just as the fate that had brought Tereza into Tomas's life was only a series of fortuitous coincidences.

In reality, this novel dedicated to lightness speaks to us above all of constraint: the web of public and private constraints that envelops people, that exercises its weight over every human relationship (and does not even spare those that Tomas would consider passing couchages). Even the Don Juanism, on which Kundera gives us a page of original definitions, has entirely other than "light" motivations: whether it be when it answers to a "lyrical obsession," which is to say it seeks among many women the unique and ideal woman, or when it is motivated by an "epic obsession," which is to say it seeks a universal knowledge in diversity.

Among the parallel stories, the most notable is that of Sabina and Franz. Sabina, as the representative of lightness and the bearer of the meanings of the book, is more persuasive than the character with whom she is contrasted, that is, Tereza. (I would say that Tereza does not succeed in having the "weight" necessary to justify a decision as self-destructive as that of Tomas.) It is through Sabina that lightness is shown to be a "semantic river," that is to say, a web of associations and images and words on which is based her amorous agreement with Tomas, a complicity that Tomas cannot find again with Tereza, or Sabina with Franz. Franz, the Swiss scientist, is the Western progressive intellectual, as can be seen by he who, from Eastern Europe, considers him with the impassive objectivity of the ethnologist studying the customs of an inhabitant of the antipodes. The vertigo of indetermination that has sustained the leftist passions of the last twenty years is indicated by Kundera with the maximum of precision compatible with so elusive an object: "The dictatorship of the proletariat or democracy? Rejection of the consumer society or demands for increased productivity? The guillotine or an end to the death penalty? It is all beside the point." What characterizes the Western left, according to Kundera, is what he calls the Grand March, which develops with the same vagueness of purpose and emotion:

> ... yesterday against the American occupation of Vietnam, today against the Vietnamese occupation of Cambodia; yesterday for Israel, today for the Palestinians; yesterday for Cuba, tomorrow against Cuba—and always against America; at times against massacres and at times in support of other massacres; Europe marches on, and to keep up with events, to leave none of them out, its pace grows faster and faster, until finally the Grand March is a procession of rushing, galloping people and the platform is shrinking and shrinking until one day it will be reduced to a mere dimensionless dot.

In accordance with the agonized imperatives of Franz's sense of duty, Kundera brings us to the threshold of the most monstrous hell generated by ideological abstractions become reality, Cambodia, and describes an international humanitarian march in pages that are a masterpiece of political satire.

At the opposite extreme of Franz, his temporary partner Sabina, by virtue of her lucid mind, acts as the author's mouthpiece, establishing comparisons and contrasts and parallels between the experience of the Communist society in which she grew up and the Western experience. One of the pivotal bases for these comparisons is the category of kitsch. Kundera explores kitsch in the sense of edulcorated, edifying, "Victorian" representation, and he thinks naturally of "socialist realism" and of political propaganda, the hypocritical mask of all horrors. Sabina, who, having established herself in the United States, loves New York for what there is there of "non-intentional beauty," "beauty by error," is upset when she sees American kitsch, Coca-Cola-like publicity, surface to remind her of the radiant images of virtue and health in which she grew up. But Kundera justly specifies:

Kitsch is the aesthetic idea of all politicians and all political parties and movements.

> Those of us who live in a society where various political tendencies exist side by side and competing influences cancel or limit one another can manage more or less to escape the kitsch inquisition.... But whenever a single political movement corners power, we find ourselves in the realm of totalitarian kitsch.

The step that remains to be taken is to free oneself of the fear of kitsch, once having saved oneself from its totalitarianism, and to be able to see it as an element among others, an image that quickly loses its own mystifying power to conserve only the color of passing time, evidence of mediocrity or of yesterday's naïumveté. This is what seems to me to happen to Sabina, in whose story we can recognize a spiritual itinerary of reconciliation with the world. At the sight, typical of the American idyll, of windows lit in a white clapboard house on a lawn, Sabina is surprised by an emotional realization. And nothing remains but for her to conclude: "No matter how we scorn it, kitsch is an integral part of the human condition."

A much sadder conclusion is that of the story of Tereza and Tomas; but here, through the death of a dog, and the obliteration of their own selves in a lost site in the country, there is almost an absorption into the cycle of nature, into an idea of the world that not only does not have man at its center, but that is absolutely not made for man.

My objections to Kundera are twofold: one terminological and one metaphysical. The terminological concerns the category of kitsch within which Kundera takes into consideration only one among many meanings. But the kitsch that claims to represent the most audacious and "cursed" broad-mindedness with facile and banal effects is also part of the bad taste of mass culture. Indeed, it is less dangerous than the other, but it must be taken into account to avoid our believing it an antidote. For example, to see the absolute contrast with kitsch in the image of a naked woman wearing a man's bowler hat does not seem to me totally convincing.

The metaphysical objection takes us farther. It regards the "categorical agreement with being," an attitude that, for Kundera, is the basis of kitsch as an aesthetic ideal. "The line separating those who doubt being as it is granted to man (no matter how or by whom) from those who accept it without reservation" resides in the fact that adherence imposes the illusion of a world in which defecation does not exist because, according to Kundera, shit is absolute metaphysical negativity. I would object that for pantheists and for the constipated (I belong to one of these two categories, though I will not specify which) defecation is one of the greatest proofs of the generosity of the universe (of nature or providence or necessity or what have you). That shit is to be considered of value and not worthless is for me a matter of principle.

From this some fundamental consequences derive. In order not to fall either into vague sentiments of a universal redemption that end up by producing monstrous police states or into generalized and temperamental pseudo-rebellions that are resolved in sheepish obedience, it is necessary to recognize how things are, whether we like them or not, both within the realm of the great, against which it is useless to struggle, and that of the small, which can be modified by our will. I believe then that a certain degree of agreement with the existent (shit included) is necessary precisely because it is incompatible with the kitsch that Kundera justly detests.

ELLEN PIFER

The Book of Laughter and Forgetting:
Kundera's Narration against Narration

In Milan Kundera's novel, *The Book of Laughter and Forgetting*, the narrator diagnoses the disease of "graphomania." "An obsession with writing books," graphomania has, he says, overtaken contemporary mass society and reached "epidemic" proportions. While graphomaniacs attempt to write their way out of the isolation induced by an advanced state of "social atomization," their obsession with self-expression paradoxically reinforces and perpetuates the sense of "general isolation" that is symptomatic of the disease. Kundera's narrator thus concludes his diagnosis: "The invention of printing originally promoted mutual understanding. In the era of graphomania the writing of books has the opposite effect: everyone surrounds himself with his own writings as with a wall of mirrors cutting off all voices from without."

Diagnosing within his own book the disease of book-writing, Kundera does more than parody the conditions under which his texts are generated and produced. Through his novel approach to novel-writing—most particularly, through the ironic voice of his narrator—he identifies, in order to subvert, some of those linguistic and cultural processes by which the writer isolates himself from others. The "wall of mirrors," cutting the writer's voice off from those "voices from without," makes obvious reference to the solipsistic tendencies of aesthetic creation and self-reflection. It recalls most directly the literary premises and practices of modernism. The

From *Journal of Narrative Technique*, Vol. 22, No. 2, Spring, 1992. © 1992 by *Journal of Narrative Technique*.

monumental narratives of Proust, Woolf, Joyce, Faulkner and others tend to dissolve the world of material and social phenomena in the medium of consciousness. Depriving Paris, Dublin or Jefferson County of any reality beyond the prisms of a character's isolated consciousness, the avatars of modernism declared the victory of imagination over the chaos of history and the ruins of time.

To those living in a less heroic literary age, Kundera's "wall of mirrors" further suggests our contemporary sense of the limitations of language and of the literary enterprise as a whole. We are reminded of what poststructuralist critics have to say about the isolation of text from world, the confinement of all writing to the "prison house of language." In contrast to the poststructuralist critic, however, this Czech novelist regards the estrangement of language, a world of signs, from the world of things as a historical rather than necessary condition. It is a condition, in Kundera's view, that the writer must vigilantly oppose, even if his resistance to these solipsistic tendencies may never wholly succeed. In his own fiction Kundera strives to create a kind of writing that, unlike the graphomaniac's, forces open a window to the world of referents beyond language and its system of signs.

The extent to which any work of narrative fiction or history can reflect actual events taking place in a world beyond language is a matter of ongoing critical debate—and I have no intention of entering this theoretical quagmire in the discussion at hand. My interest lies, rather, in the way that Kundera's vision of the novelistic enterprise, and of the novelist's obligations to a world of referents beyond the self and language, governs his narrative methods and practice. This is not to say, however, that Kundera's view of language is nostalgic or naive. Breaking through the "wall of mirrors"—unlocking the circle of the self—exposes both the writer and his readers to uncertainty. To admit the world is to admit ambiguity, contingency, irony—above all, to question. As Kundera has said on more than one occasion, the novel's task is not to answer questions but to raise them. Scrupulously practicing what he preaches, this novelist disrupts conventional narrative structure and sabotages the writer's authority in order to interrogate the text. Sprinkling his narration with rhetorical questions, countering an "obvious explanation" with one he finds "more convincing," the author's narrating persona exposes both the characters and their author to skeptical scrutiny.

In the opening section of *The Book of Laughter and Forgetting*, for example, the narrator confronts his readers with a question: why, he asks, is Mirek, an intellectual whose history is being recounted here, so ashamed of an affair he had, twenty-five years ago, with an "ugly" woman named Zdena? The narrator offers an "obvious explanation" that he immediately retracts, because he doesn't "find it convincing enough." Reluctantly he admits the more convincing explanation, which also proves less flattering to the male ego: cowardly and insecure in his youth, Mirek had "taken an ugly mistress because he didn't dare go after beautiful women."

In his subsequent attempt to remove all traces, all record of his (now humiliating) three-year affair with Zdena, Mirek has, the narrator points out, set himself up as an author—claiming the rights of any novelist over his material. "One of a novelist's inalienable rights," the narrator states, "is to be able to rework his novel. If he takes a dislike to the beginning, he can rewrite it or cross it out entirely." Unfortunately, when Zdena reappears on the scene, Mirek is forced to confront the discomfiting fact that this woman is not his own invention. Kundera's narrator slyly comments: "But Zdena's existence deprived Mirek of his prerogative as an author. Zdena insisted on remaining part of the opening pages of the novel. She refused to be crossed out." While Mirek remains the focus of Kundera's satire here, the author is not above satirizing his own enterprise as well. Novelists will always claim the right to "rework" their novels for the sake of style, structure and effect. Still, the writer's efforts to provide a seamless work of art—ironing out the unsightly wrinkles caused by human nature and history—may implicate him in the same criticism levelled at Mirek. Foregrounding the processes by which the novelist rewrites and revises his material, Kundera undermines the illusion that his text is either timeless or impersonal. As Ann Banfield observes in her study, *Unspeakable Sentences*, "Only in writing [as opposed to speaking] may the process of revision, which is part of the process of composition, vanish in the finished piece, the 'clean copy,' leaving no sign of what the first or any intervening versions may have looked like." By calling attention to the erasure of those telling "signs" of revision, Kundera undermines the effects by which the written text appears to transcend the ephemeral and contingent conditions of its own production.

"Écriture," Banfield explains in another study, "is the name for the coming to language of a knowledge, whether objective or subjective, which is not personal." Resisting the notion of writing's impersonality—a notion that, as Banfield points out, French writers from Flaubert to Foucault have sought to emphasize—Kundera flagrantly inserts his personal biography into the narrative. Enlisting his narrating persona as guide, goad and agent provocateur, Kundera draws attention not only to the author behind the text but to the way that personal experience motivates the act of writing. "Why is Tamina on a children's island?" asks the narrator of *The Book of Laughter and Forgetting*. "Why is that where I imagine her?" His answer characteristically fails to provide a definite answer. "I don't know," he admits, adding: "Maybe it's because on the day my father died the air was full of joyful songs sung by children's voices."

Undermining the illusion of "knowledge" that écriture creates, Kundera would open his text to uncertainty as well as the personal. Interspersing what Gerald Prince calls "signs of the 'you'" throughout the novel, Kundera's narrator repeatedly addresses and queries the narratee—the "you" implicitly or explicitly being addressed. In this way he opens the text not only to question but, in Prince's phrase, to "another world" outside the novel and its characters, which is "known to both the narrator and the narratee." Enlisting a narrating persona who shares this "other world" and all its problematic conditions with the reader, Kundera abandons the covert operations of an omniscient creator for the overt strategies of a self-conscious narrator.

By inserting his personal background and history into the text, Kundera is not building a "wall of mirrors" around himself as writing subject. Instead, he employs the biographical persona, like the other narrative devices characteristic of his art, to open a window (both literally and figuratively) on the political history of Czechoslovakia and on the invented history of his characters. In *The Book of Laughter and Forgetting*, for example, the narrator identifies the "joyful" tune sung by "children's voices" on the day Kundera's father died as the "Internationale": "Everywhere east of the Elbe," he explains, "children are banded together in what are called Pioneer organizations" that teach them to become good communists. On the day that Kundera's father died, Gustav Husak—installed by the Russians in 1969 as the seventh president of Czechoslovakia—received an award from these children's groups. At "a festive ceremony in Prague Castle," the narrator tells us, Husak, "the president of forgetting," is "being named an Honorary Pioneer." At the end of the ceremony, the President's words, amplified over the loudspeaker, drift in through the very window of the room where Kundera's father lies dying: "Children! You are the future!" Husak proclaims. "Children! Never look back!"

Here the author's personal loss, the death of his beloved father, serves as yet another variation on the theme of "forgetting" that informs each section of the novel. The erosion of memory that constitutes Tamina's personal tragedy is identified with the author's personal tragedy and, on a larger scale, with the tragedy of Czechoslovakia under totalitarian rule. In Kundera's unsentimental vision, moreover, children serve as emblems of the mindless "infantocracy" overtaking contemporary culture in both East and West. In the oblivious consciousness of childhood, devoid of past and memory, the author perceives the dire future of postindustrial society.

Because, as the narrator later points out, children "have no past whatsoever," they bear no "burden of memory"; hence "childhood is the image of the future." In Western technocracy's enslavement to the blandishments of mass media as well as in Eastern Europe's seventy-year subjugation to totalitarian rule, Kundera detects the same mindless faith in the future. Wooed by the urge to escape history and its burdens, contemporary culture risks losing not only its collective memory but the very source of individual identity.

Calling attention to the biographical author, his history, and the temporal processes that help to erode as well as create written artifacts, Kundera stresses the connection not only between author and text, but between language and identity. The reliance of human and cultural identity upon language, and of language upon memory, is a central theme in The *Book of Laughter and Forgetting*—a theme succinctly dramatized by the ten-year illness that proves fatal for Kundera's father. One major symptom of this disease is the gradual erosion of memory, which causes his father to lose "the power of speech" and ultimately the ability to write a coherent text. "At first," the narrator says, his father "simply had trouble calling up certain words or would say similar words instead and then immediately laugh at himself. In the end he had only a handful of words left.... Things lost their names and merged into a single, undifferentiated reality. I was the only one who by talking to him could temporarily transform that nameless infinity into the world of clearly named entities." In the end, the father's "memory lapses" become so fierce that the dying man has to abandon his "study of Beethoven's sonatas"; "no one," the narrator explains, "could understand the text." The father's writing, like his speech, becomes an incomprehensible jumble: an impersonal void or "nameless infinity" of "undifferentiated" language.

It is through language, Kundera reminds us, that we name or identify not only things but ourselves. Identity, like meaning in a text, arises from difference; and the ability to differentiate one word from another—or one thing, one event, one person, one author, one culture from another— depends on memory. Memory of the past, recorded as history, keeps alive our sense of differentiation and identity; it prevents us from slipping into the "nameless infinity" of "undifferentiated reality." As the novelist's character Tamina comes to realize, "the sum total of her being is no more than what she sees in the distance, behind her. And as her past begins to shrink, disappear, fall apart, Tamina begins shrinking and blurring" as well.

Such "shrinking and blurring," Kundera suggests, befalls each of us as we age, lose our faculties and slowly surrender to oblivion. Not only does the

aging Mother, in Part Two of *The Book of Laughter and Forgetting*, begin to
lose her sight—she loses her memory and with it her experience of history:

> One night, for example, the tanks of a huge neighboring
> country [as Kundera's narrator puts it] came and occupied their
> country. The shock was so great, so terrible, that for a long time
> no one could think about anything else. It was August, and the
> pears in their garden were nearly ripe. The week before, Mother
> had invited the local pharmacist to come and pick them. He never
> came, never apologized. The fact that Mother refused to forgive
> him drove [her son] Karel and [his wife] Marketa crazy.
> Everybody's thinking about tanks, and all you can think about is
> pears, they yelled.

Karel's old Mother, the narrator suggests, has "moved on to the
different world" of a second childhood. She has joined "a different order of
creature: smaller, lighter, more easily blown away."

Whereas an old woman's second childhood appears natural and even
comic, notwithstanding the announcement of death that it brings, Tamina's
fate is truly tragic. A young woman exiled from her country and all that she
loves, Tamina slides into premature death when she is brought to an island
"wilderness" populated by children. There, surrounded by these tiny beings
who have no past, no memory, no history, she is consigned to oblivion. On
this remote "children's island," Tamina confronts a world hostile to privacy,
individuation or difference. "We're all children here!" the youthful
inhabitants gleefully shout. Held captive like Gulliver among the
Lilliputians, Tamina tries but fails to escape. Making a run for the shore, she
spies the children dancing together in a clearing and takes refuge "behind the
thick trunk of a plane tree." From this hiding place she watches the children
jerk and gyrate to the rhythms of rock music, the din of amplified guitars
blaring from a tape recorder set down in the middle of the clearing. "The
lewdness of the motions superimposed on their children's bodies," Kundera's
narrator observes, "destroys the dichotomy between obscenity and
innocence, purity and corruption. Sensuality loses all its meaning, innocence
loses all its meaning, words fall apart." Once again taking language as his
paradigm, Kundera links the forces of forgetting with the death of difference.

Pitting memory against oblivion, Kundera's novels celebrate difference
at every level—starting with the systematic polarities by which language
operates to create meaning. Each of these novels, moreover, typically
incorporates a variety of types or modes of discourse within its narrative.

Interspersing the fictional histories of his characters with passages devoted to philosophical speculation, historical commentary, and even quotations from other published and unpublished texts, Kundera makes contrast or difference both a structural and a thematic principle. The overall effect of this counterpoint is to dispel the intensity of any single, or single-voiced, narration. By disrupting the seamless effects of narration, Kundera wakens his readers from the "spell" cast by art and confronts them with the burden of history. "We who remember," his narrator tells us in *Life Is Elsewhere*, "must bear witness."

Just as Flaubert employed the devices of realism to undercut Emma Bovary's romantic reveries—and created, in the process, a novel about the dangers of reading novels—so Kundera, at a later stage of the novel's development, employs the self-conscious devices of postmodernist narrative to subvert the lyric spell of his own narration. "Lyrical poetry," he has said, "is a realm in which any statement immediately becomes truth. Yesterday the poet said life is a vale of tears; today he said life is a land of smiles; and he was right both times. There is no inconsistency. The lyrical poet does not have to prove anything. The only proof is the intensity of his own emotions." The novelist, on the other hand, must assume the burden of history and, therefore, of "proof." The distinction Kundera draws between novels and lyric poetry further suggests why so much of his own writing is devoted to speculation and argument. And while the novelist endeavors, through his narrating persona, to present certain conclusions, as well as questions, with vigor and force, this persona also reminds Kundera's readers that the author is no prophet or visionary. Declining the role of omniscient creator, he is simply another limited mortal caught in "the trap" of history. As such, he enlists in his narrative not only the voice of his biographical persona but the timely voices of the author's friends and family, of Czech officials and world leaders, of current dogmas and classic works of literature.

The devices of narrative reflexivity are, paradoxically, the means by which Kundera lays siege to the graphomaniac's self-absorbed, self-reflecting "wall of mirrors." It is in the "mirrored house of poetry," moreover, that Kundera locates this "wall of mirrors" and its isolating effects. Drawing a distinction between novels and poetry that recalls Bakhtin's theory of discourse in *The Dialogic Imagination*, Kundera celebrates the novel's hybrid language and structure—contrasting the formal freedoms of this genre with the strictures of poetry and its compulsively "lyric attitude." But with freedom comes responsibility; the novel, unlike the poem, is answerable to history. What Kundera's narrator says of his character Tamina, who makes a scrupulous record of her past in order to oppose the forces of forgetting, may also be said of her author: "She has no desire to turn the past into poetry, she wants to give the past back its lost body. She is not compelled by a desire for beauty, she is compelled by a desire for life."

This distinction between poetry and life, beauty and history, informs all of Kundera's fiction. In *The Book of Laughter and Forgetting*, Tamina's efforts to retrieve, with all its ugliness, the past's "lost body" are contrasted with Karel's preference for poetic oblivion. Earlier in the novel, Karel rhapsodically muses over the stages of his bygone youth. Rather than strive "to give the past back its lost body," he begins to manipulate—and even to dismember—that elusive body for his own gratification. As Karel projects his desire upon the past, conjuring an "idyllic landscape" that never existed, his author likens him to "a collage artist, cutting out part of one engraving and pasting it over another." Taking delight in his finished creation, Karel gratefully contemplates the transcendent power of art: "Beauty," he reflects, "is a clean sweep of chronology, a rebellion against time."

Not only in this passage but throughout the novel Kundera invites us to contemplate the difference between the operation of historical memory— our urgent efforts to retrieve and preserve what has transpired in our experience, no matter how painful or daunting the task—and the immemorial desire of human beings "to turn the past into poetry." "History," as his narrator later remarks, "is a succession of ephemeral changes. Eternal values exist outside history. They are immutable and have no need of memory." Human memory—in contrast to Apollo's lyre—is a mortal rather than divine attribute; and those who exercise it must serve time. Those of us who seek to remember, to "bear witness," must acknowledge contingency in the very act of giving "the past back its lost body." Invoking "chronology" and the ephemeral at every turn, Kundera's skeptical, antimodernist version of narrative undermines the quest for transcendence. Precisely because they are so time-laden, his novels announce "the unbearable lightness of being."

While Kundera's distinction between poetry and prose, art and life sheds light on his enterprise as a novelist, it would be misleading to regard the distinction he draws as absolute. In the preface to his novel, *Life Is Elsewhere*, the author identifies the relationship of poetry to his own works of prose. In composing this novel, Kundera says, he wanted "to solve an esthetic problem: how to write a novel which would be a 'critique of poetry' and yet at the same time would itself be poetry"—would, that is, "transmit poetic intensity and imagination." Only by "catching [an] image" in the depths of its own linguistic "mirrors," he later suggests, can a novel be said to reflect or represent reality. Like most novelists since Cervantes, Kundera registers a fertile ambivalence about his obligations to art, on the one hand, and to history or actuality on the other. What merits particular attention in his case is the way that his narrative isolates and foregrounds its aesthetic or "lyric" impulse in order to undermine the spell that it casts.

It was Edmund Wilson, writing over half a century ago in *Axel's Castle*, who first cautioned readers about the tendency of modernist writers to abandon the novelist's traditional, and salutary, ambivalence toward the seductive power of imagination. Expressing admiration for Proust's formidable accomplishments in *A la recherché du temps perdu*, Wilson nonetheless offers a critical reservation: "The fascination of Proust's novel is so great that, while we are reading it, we tend to accept it in toto. In convincing us of the reality of his creations, Proust infects us with his point of view, even where his point of view has falsified his picture of life." Now, to charge a work of fiction with "falsification" may strike some readers— particularly if they are students of narrative theory—as paradoxical, if not confused. The difference between novels and history, Banfield maintains in *Unspeakable Sentences*, "is that the fictional narrative statement is immune to judgments of truth or falsity; in fiction, they are suspended. Rather, it [fiction] creates by fiat a fictional reality which can only be taken as fictionally true."

Nevertheless, as Wilson's comment on Proust's "falsification" makes clear, even the most sophisticated readers of narrative fiction may implicitly acknowledge the novelist's traditional obligations to truth or history. Thomas Leitch, in a theoretical study entitled "What Stories Are," is more willing to acknowledge the blurred border between fictional and nonfictional narrative, allowing that it is "a difference in emphasis." The "success or failure of a work of history," says Leitch, clearly depends on the status of the implicated propositions" it makes. By contrast, novels—even those that "may propose implicated explanations of historical events"—do not display the same degree of "this commitment." That is why, we might add, Edmund Wilson can both admire Proust's novel and find it guilty of "falsification." Wilson would certainly employ more stringent criteria, or "judgments of truth," when assessing the work of a French historian of the same period.

Still, as Banfield herself points out, the fiction writer's power to create a world "by fiat" can be viewed as a liability by novelists seeking to uphold their obligations to history. The fiction writer, Banfield says, can neither "tell the truth" nor "write a sentence of narration which is false"—which, in other words, "can be taken by readers of novels as false. His or hers is the midas touch which turns all fiction, that is, to fictional truth, and thereby abolishes all distinctions between the true and the false." By insisting, stylistically and thematically, upon the novel's burden of "proof," Kundera would deliver his readers from the "midas touch" of narrative art. By interrogating his text—inviting the reader to question and debate the narrator's assertions—he overtly appeals to those "distinctions between the true and the false" of which Banfield judges the novel incapable. To distinguish a statement of truth from a "lie," Banfield says, there must be "a communication to an interlocutor." Perhaps that is why Kundera insists that his readers adopt the role of interlocutor. He would guard against the hypnotic spell of narrative—the power of Proust's novel to transform, midas-like, the false into the true—and offer, instead, a critique of that power to which all novels, including his own, nonetheless aspire. By curbing the degree of "infection" that "poetic intensity and imagination" visit upon the novel's readers, Kundera would lift the quarantine that seals contemporary writing in a "wall of mirrors" and denies the novelist healthy exposure to history and its "judgments of truth."

The liberties Kundera takes with the categories of fiction and nonfiction, narrative and essay—the way he flagrantly juxtaposes historical reportage and documentary with the symbolic landscape of fantasy and fable—signals his commitment to the political as well as formal freedoms he perceives in the novel-genre. This is hardly surprising for a writer who regards the aesthetic and political processes as springing from a common source and operating according to the same human laws. "The metaphysics of man," he maintains, "is the same in the private sphere as in the public one."

In the "lyric attitude" of the poet Kundera identifies the same totalizing urge, the same desire to create or transform reality in toto, that fosters human faith in a cosmic order or in sundry ideologies promising paradise on earth. The same impulse that compels the poet or writer to seek immortality in song, perfection in art, leads to the creation of larger allied and alloyed structures, including grandiose political schemes. When society allows itself to be carried away by "the lyric attitude," constructing an ideal or "idyll" of absolute order and harmony, for example, the quest ends in collective disaster. That is why Kundera refers to Czechoslovakia's era of communist repression—an "era of political trials, persecutions, forbidden books, and legalized murder"—as "not only an epoch of terror, but also an epoch of lyricism, ruled hand in hand by the hangman and the poet." Desire for absolute order in the social sphere, like insistence upon absolute truth or meaning in the linguistic, leads to repression. "The impulse to totalization," as Hazard Adams and Leroy Searle summarize Derrida's argument, is linked to "the totalitarian.... The desire for closure, as guarantor of meaning and intelligibility, becomes the instrumentality of repression."

Observing a similar connection between the totalizing and totalitarian impulse but developing its implications well beyond the linguistic, Kundera tells an interviewer: "Totalitarianism is not only hell, but also the dream of paradise—the age-old dream of a world where everybody would live in harmony, united by a single common will and faith.... The whole period of Stalinist terror was a period of collective lyrical delirium." He adds, "hell is already contained in the dream of paradise and if we wish to understand the essence of hell we must examine the essence of the paradise from which it originated. It is extremely easy to condemn gulags, but to reject the totalitarian poesy which leads to the gulag by way of paradise is as difficult as ever." When the "lyric attitude" spills over from art to life, Kundera suggests, it may take disastrous social and political forms. Fleeing from contingency, desiring to escape the burden of memory and history, the utopian dreamer embraces a nonexistent future, attempting to realize paradise—a perfect world of order, harmony and "eternal values"—on earth.

The consequences, Kundera warns, are dangerous if not fatal: "Once the dream of paradise starts to turn into reality, however, here and there people begin to crop up who stand in its way, and so the rulers of paradise must build a little gulag on the side of Eden. In the course of time this gulag grows ever bigger and more perfect, while the adjoining paradise gets ever smaller and poorer." The structure is maintained through violence; elements that cannot or will not join the happy circle must be cast out, consigned to the prisons and torture chambers devised by those in charge. The totalitarian hell gradually subsumes its putative heaven.

The implications of Kundera's secular version of heaven and hell are grim. But the dire nature of these observations belies their bracing comic effect in the novels, tricked out as they are by the narrator's characteristic lightness of delivery. Nowhere is this combination of deft narration and dark inference more apparent, and effective, than in the final scene of *The Book of Laughter and Forgetting*. The novel draws to a close on the private beach of "an abandoned island" somewhere on the Adriatic, where a small resort hotel caters to vacationers. The island and its shoreline offer a kind of realistic counterpoint to that symbolic wilderness, the "children's island," from which Tamina, earlier in the novel, tries to escape. On the latter island, the symbolic circle of identical children is supplanted by a population of vacationing nudists equally uniform in their nakedness: "They went naked down the steps to the beach, where other naked people were sitting in groups, taking walks, and swimming—naked mothers and naked children, naked grandmothers and naked grandchildren, the naked young and the naked elderly."

Surrounded by this anonymous population, Kundera's protagonists, a young man named Jan and his girlfriend Edwige, make friends with a smaller "group of naked people," all of whom have come to this "natural paradise" seeking to rid themselves of "the hypocrisy of a society that cripples body and soul." By casting off their clothing, the group collectively embraces the ideal of natural freedom, of living "at one with nature." A theory advanced by one member of the group, "a man with an extraordinary paunch," formulates their collective ideal and goal: to "be freed once and for all from the bonds of Judeo-Christian thought." The idyll of "perfect harmony," perfect freedom, "perfect solidarity" requires that the accumulated legacy of the past—the traditions, norms, structures and systems of a civilization, the cultural language by which its members have identified themselves to one another and themselves—be not altered but erased. "Eternal values," as Kundera's narrator has already observed, "exist outside history."

In the nudists' shared dream of a "natural paradise" we detect the "collective lyrical delirium" that in Kundera's view governs all utopian heavens, giving rise in turn to the hell latent in each artificial paradise. As Jan gazes at the mass of naked bodies scattered along the shore, he has a dark inkling of the connection between earthly notions of heaven and the various forms of hell to which they lead. Made "melancholy" by the spectacle of so much undifferentiated, "meaningless" flesh, Jan is suddenly "overwhelmed by a strange feeling of affliction, and from that haze of affliction came an even stranger thought: that the Jews had filed into Hitler's gas chambers naked and en masse." Jan is led to consider the possibility that "nudity" is itself a kind of "uniform." Here Kundera's language evokes a suggestive connection between the Jews' uniform nakedness and the uniforms of their Nazi exterminators. Unable to bear "the sight of all those naked bodies on the beach," Jan suddenly arrives at the startling notion "that nudity is a shroud."

Bewitched by a particularly virulent strain of "totalitarian poesy," the German nature participated in the dream of an Aryan paradise—and stoked the hellish fires of the gas chambers. Genocide, the attempt to erase a people and their history from the face of the earth, is one outgrowth of that totalizing impulse, or "collective lyrical delirium," which makes the nude bathers so eager to free themselves of the fetters of the past. To erase the memory of an admittedly troubled and imperfect history leads not to a brave new world, however, but to the loss of human differentiation and identity. Mass murder, mass extinction, Kundera suggests, is simply the dark fulfillment of mankind's oblivious dream of utopia.

The sunlight that shines on the closing scene of *The Book of Laughter and Forgetting* is tinged with dark irony. The small circle of nudists standing together on the sand look harmless enough as they congratulate themselves on their temporary freedom from the "civilization" that "imprisons" them. But then the man whose single distinguishing feature is that "extraordinary paunch" begins to extol the future and its promised liberation from the strictures of the past. As the group attends to what the paunchy man is saying, Kundera draws this scene and his novel to a close: "On and on the man talked. The others listened with interest, their naked genitals staring dully, sadly, listlessly at the yellow sand." More eloquent than any words the nudists can muster is the limp expression of their exposed genitals. Like domestic pets suddenly turned loose from their leashes, these naked organs appear bewildered by their abrupt and unexpected release from bondage; something more than mere clothing appears to have been discarded. Exposed to the harsh glare of daylight, the nudists' bodies inadvertently register the oblivion into which they have been cast: the hell of "undifferentiated reality." The pride of their once private parts has mysteriously vanished with the clothing that constrained them. The body's sudden liberation from social "bonds," from all the trappings of civilization, consigns these sad appendages to the same flaccid existence that, Kundera wittily suggests, the mind's longed-for deliverance from a binding system of difference, linguistic and cultural, would entail.

Sustaining a polyphony of light and dark themes, personal and public voices, Kundera takes full advantage of what he calls the "synthetic power of the novel." By coming at his "subject from all sides," as he puts it, the novelist combines "ironic essay, novelistic narrative, autobiographical fragment, historic fact, flight of fantasy." The culminating effect is not of closure but of equilibrium, like the contrapuntal harmony created by "the voices of polyphonic music." The musical analogy is one that Kundera consistently favors. In *The Book of Laughter and Forgetting*, his narrator draws an instructive parallel between the novel's structure and the "journey of the variation form" in music. "This entire book," he announces, "is a novel in the form of variations." Likening his narrative to the voyage of discovery Beethoven undertook, Kundera hints at the special attraction that this mode of exploration holds for a novelist attempting to cure himself of the disease of graphomania. "What Beethoven discovered in his variations," the novel's narrator points out, "was another space and direction"—"the infinity of internal variety concealed in all things."

Structuring his novel on a set of stylistic and thematic variations, Kundera, like Beethoven, seeks "another space and direction." It is another space and direction not only because the territory is new but because it lies beyond the isolated self, outside the "wall of mirrors" enclosing the writer in endless self-reflections. The writer liberates himself by liberating his readers: he does not carry us away in the mesmerizing flow of narrated events or in a lyric flight so compelling that it cannot be examined and resisted. Instead of cutting off our "voices from without," he opens up the text to query and debate. To clear this ground or mental "space" for the reader, Kundera develops his narration, structurally and thematically, as an ongoing process of interrogation, differentiation and contrast. Differentiation discovers a virtually endless variety of entities and identities, of contrasting forms, patterns and poles of meaning. The "polyphonic" text disrupts the flow of narration, cancels its lyric impetus, by juxtaposing unlike elements that insistently retain their discrete and contrary identities. Juxtaposing these contrasting elements—interrogating one tone, stance, concept or style with another as the narrative swerves between sexual high jinks and high seriousness—Kundera's text resists the solipsistic forces that drive its production. Turning the art of narration against itself, the author creates a novel that is at once an artful manifestation of "graphomania" and his bracing attempt at a cure.

JAMES S. HANS

Kundera's Laws of Beauty

Milan Kundera's novel *The Unbearable Lightness of Being* provides a serious revision of our conceptions of the nature of beauty, and in so doing it forces us to reconsider the relationship between the aesthetic and our daily lives. At the same time, the novel itself reflects the changes Kundera has brought about via his Nietzschean assessment of forms. Part traditional fiction, part essay, part lyrical exclamation, *The Unbearable Lightness of Being* is a decidedly impure form, one that celebrates its mixed heritage even as it establishes an essential relationship between shame and beauty. In addressing the linkages between the beautiful and the shameful, the novel also registers the ways in which our attitude toward these most fundamental regions of human existence affect our political disposition as well, for Kundera demonstrates throughout the book that even as all human relationships have something to do with questions of power, so too do the manifestations of power reflect the individual's attitude toward his or her sense of beauty and shame. The ultimate effect of all these revisions of the basic categories of human experience is to raise again the question that Nietzsche first posed for us, to ask us once more what it means to be wholly human, what it would mean if we were finally capable of accepting existence on the terms through which it presents itself to us.

From *Essays in Literature*, Vol. XIX, No. 1, Spring, 1992. © 1992 by *Essays in Literature*.

Kundera's most striking appraisal of beauty occurs early in the novel when he is discussing the relationship between coincidences in life and in fiction. He has established that his two main characters, Tomas and Tereza, have met through a series of rather mundane fortuities and thereby irrevocably changed their lives, and this prompts him to discuss the great importance of chance on the outcome of our individual fates:

> Much more than the card he slipped her at the last minute, it was the call of all those fortuities (the book, Beethoven, the number six, the yellow park bench) which gave her [Tereza] the courage to leave home and change her fate. It may well be those few fortuities (quite modest, by the way, even drab, just what one would expect from so lackluster a town) which set her love in motion and provided her with a source of energy she had not yet exhausted at the end of her days.

Our day-to-day life is bombarded with fortuities, or, to be more precise, with the accidental meetings of people and events we call coincidences. "Coincidence" means that two events unexpectedly happen at the same time, they meet: Tomas appears in the hotel restaurant at the same time the radio is playing Beethoven. We do not even notice the great majority of such coincidences. If the seat Tomas occupied had been occupied instead by the local butcher, Tereza never would have noticed that the radio was playing Beethoven (though the meeting of Beethoven and the butcher would also have been an interesting coincidence). But her nascent love inflamed her sense of beauty, and she would never forget that music. Whenever she heard it, she would be touched. Everything going on around her at that moment would be haloed by the music and take on its beauty.

According to our traditional ways of thinking, the kinds of fortuities that prompt Tereza to take an interest in Tomas—and those that prompt him to be interested in her—are not to be taken seriously. We all know how seemingly unrelated things can come together during the initial moments of important relationships, and we tend to denigrate their importance. These coincidences may enhance the memory of first meetings and the like a bit, but they are not to be taken seriously precisely because of their idiosyncratic nature. Tereza would be most foolish to assert that her love for Tomas was important because it was linked from the beginning with the music of Beethoven, or the number six, or books, or park benches. Yet that is precisely what Kundera argues here.

The initial meeting between Tereza and Tomas prompts us to pay more attention to the fortuities in our own lives, for if Kundera can assert that the small coincidences in Tereza's life may well have "set her love in motion and provided her with a source of energy she had not yet exhausted at the end of her days," we must assume that such events can have great power both to transform and to sustain our lives. Why, then, do we tend to disregard them so much? Why act as though these coincidences are largely unrelated to the outcomes of our lives? And why do we in turn expect our writers of narrative fiction to keep the fortuities in their stories to a minimum? Without directly explaining why, Kundera tells us what we are missing when we ignore them:

> Early in the novel that Tereza clutched under her arm when she went to visit Tomas, Anna meets Vronsky in curious circumstances: they are at the railway station when someone is run over by a train. At the end of the novel, Anna throws herself under a train. This symmetrical composition—the same motif appears at the beginning and at the end—may seem quite "novelistic" to you, and I am willing to agree, but only on condition that you refrain from reading such notions as "fictive," "fabricated," and "untrue to life" into the word "novelistic." Because human lives are composed in precisely such a fashion.

They are composed like music. Guided by his sense of beauty, an individual transforms a fortuitous occurrence (Beethoven's music, death under a train) into a motif, which then assumes a permanent place in the composition of the individual's life. Anna could have chosen another way to take her life. But the motif of death and the railway station, unforgettably bound to the birth of love, enticed her in her hour of despair with its dark beauty. Without realizing it, the individual composes his life according to the laws of beauty even in times of greatest distress.

It is wrong, then, to chide the novel for being fascinated by mysterious coincidences (like the meeting of Anna, Vronsky, the railway station, and death or the meeting of Beethoven, Tomas, Tereza, and the cognac), but it is right to chide man for being blind to such coincidences in his daily life. For he thereby deprives his life of a dimension of beauty.

Turning the tables on us, Kundera argues that instead of criticizing him for building a relationship between his characters out of such flimsy coincidences, we ourselves are to be faulted for failing to recognize the ways in which similar fortuities shape our own lives.

More importantly, Kundera establishes the fundamental premise of the novel by asserting: "Without realizing it, the individual composes his life according to the laws of beauty even in times of greatest distress." Instead of creating our lives out of a series of rational considerations about what we should be doing that would be based on various considerations for the future, here we are told that instead we compose our lives according to the laws of beauty. And we do this without realizing it. First and foremost, Kundera has shifted the control of our lives away from any self-aware context and moved it to another location that does its work without any necessary reflection on our part. Unlike Freud's unconscious, though, this location construes our lives in terms of the laws of beauty, a phrase that marks out a considerably different space from one like "libidinal urges" or "the pleasure principle." The motifs in Tereza's life—Beethoven's music, reading books, the number six—have nothing to do with sexual energy per se any more than they concentrate exclusively on the pursuit of pleasure. These are ordering processes that differ precisely because they are self-centered, because they reflect only the interests of the libido or the unconscious forces that urge us into one mode of pleasure-seeking or another. The laws of beauty would by definition be something beyond mere self-interest, something that adds another dimension to our lives rather than something that reduces them to the endless expression of libidinal energies.

Not that Tomas and Tereza don't have active libidos, for they most surely do. Nor is the implication of "the laws of beauty" that sexual and bodily activity in general take a subordinate place to "higher" forms of human expression. On the contrary, the laws of beauty work themselves out most pertinently in sexual and bodily contexts, situations that are not to be separated from Beethoven's music or Tolstoy's novels. If body and soul are not always in accord—as Tereza's rumbling stomach emphasizes—the laws according to which they both operate remain the same, even if we fail too often to recognize this to be so.

Nevertheless, when one considers the fortuities that brought Tereza and Tomas together, "laws of beauty" seems a rather excessive term to apply to them. It is not just that they are fortuities but that they are such slight and meaningless ones. Even Kundera emphasizes their drabness, and their highly idiosyncratic nature seems to deny any linkage to a law, even if in some respects they might have some connection to beauty. The logic of Tereza's interest in Beethoven, for example, is skewed from the beginning, for there is no indication that she properly appreciates the value of the music itself. Instead, she values Beethoven because he symbolizes something "higher" to her, and yet this "higher" sensibility comes not from what others might have suggested about the greatness of his work but rather from the fact that his music was associated with a context that had nothing to do with the music per se. Tereza had known his music from the time a string quartet from Prague had visited their town. Tereza (who, as we know, yearned for "something higher") went to the concert. The hall was nearly empty. The only other people in the audience were the local pharmacist and his wife. And although the quartet of musicians on stage faced only a trio of spectators down below, they were kind enough not to cancel the concert, and gave a private performance of the last three Beethoven quartets.

Then the pharmacist invited the musicians to dinner and asked the girl in the audience to come along with them. From then on, Beethoven became her image of the world on the other side, the world she yearned for.

If there is beauty here, it has little to do with an aesthetic appreciation of Beethoven's last quartets. Beethoven himself may rightly symbolize in some fashion "something higher," but just what that "something higher" is remains located instead in the special privilege of the private performance of the musicians and the invitation to the pharmacist's house, hardly the sort of things that have to do with beauty.

It is worth noting that as a result of Tereza's interest in Beethoven, Tomas too attends to his music, and consequently Tomas himself establishes one of his own motifs on the basis of "the difficult resolution" to be found in the "Es muss sein" motif in Beethoven's last quartet; it is thus possible for the patterns one establishes on the basis of pure idiosyncracy to bear resemblance finally to their original source. Likewise, it is "co-incidental" in this way that Tereza's rather frivolous use of Beethoven's music becomes more serious when it is connected to Tomas's difficult decision to return to Prague and Tereza, for, as Kundera tells us, the same thing originally happened to the "Es muss sein" formula for Beethoven, which was once part of a humorous anecdote concerning a debt that was owed to Beethoven but was in the end turned into the weighty resolution of the last quartet. These fortuities suggest something beyond mere coincidence, or at the very least offer the possibility that one grows into the full consequences of the coincidences that give shape to one's life.

If we are to take the laws of beauty seriously, though, we have to assume that it doesn't matter that Teresa doesn't understand fully the beauty of Beethoven's music. The laws of beauty as they manifest themselves in her life don't necessarily have anything at all to do with the music, even if the music itself symbolizes "something higher." This is made clear by the complete frivolity of some of the other coincidences connected to Tereza's first meeting with Tomas, particularly the yellow park bench and the number six.

Neither the bench nor the number six has anything that intrinsically connects it to beauty; the linkage is a purely idiosyncratic one based on Tereza's life, derived from the emerging motifs that have been established in her past. She herself has conferred special values on these things, and when they turn up again in contexts that may well have further significance for her, their value is increased yet again. The individual items in the motif are, we might say, totally arbitrary. There is nothing in the number six that gives it special value; its value comes only from its place within the lived experience that Tereza places it in, derives from its coincidental connection in her mind with something important in her life. But the pattern that is established on the basis of these arbitrary linkages reflects the laws of beauty and demonstrates the way patterns and motifs are inevitably developed in any domain, regardless of their idiosyncratic origins.

The "Es muss sein" of Beethoven reflects this process very well, for the original context, we could say, is totally idiosyncratic. Beethoven is owed some money, he needs the money and therefore asks the debtor if he can give it to him, and the man asks "Muss es sein?" To which, Kundera tells us, "Beethoven replied, with a hearty laugh, 'Es muss sein!' and immediately jotted down these words and their melody." But the melody is hardly the serious one of the last quartet: "On this realistic motif he then composed a canon for four voices: three voices sing 'Es muss sein, es muss sein, ja, ja, ja!' (It must be, it must be, yes, yes, yes, yes!), and the fourth voice chimes in with 'Heraus mit dem Beutel!' (Out with the purse!)."

This jocular request for money is far from the difficult resolution of the last quartet, and yet there is no reason why the phrase "Es muss sein" should not take on another cast later in Beethoven's life and become a heavier motif about weighty decisions. The phrase itself first has significance only because Beethoven chooses to note it and turn it back on its originator, thereby making fun of the rather serious response to a minor request, and in this way it has no more weight than any other phrase one might pick out of another's conversation to play with. But that idiosyncratic beginning establishes the phrase as a musical motif in Beethoven's life, to which he can return at a later date and translate into a more serious musical enterprise.

Tereza's and Tomas's lives, then, are composed according to the laws of beauty, which means that the coincidental things their own particular situation prompts them to attend to become motifs that reflect the general patterns of beauty and the motifs out of which all aesthetic aspects of the world are constructed. There are laws to their behavior, even if those laws coincide with the purely gratuitous elements of their lives that fate throws in their paths, and those laws give their lives all the beauty they will ever have. Kundera suggests through these characters' lives that our existence is fundamentally aesthetic in nature, even if we fail to recognize this, even if we assume that we are always in rational control of the direction of our lives. Again, he emphasizes that "the individual composes his life according to the laws of beauty even in times of greatest distress," when beauty would be the last thing one would likely think about. And again, Kundera does not say that we compose our lives according to the pleasure principle, or on the basis of libidinal flows or the desire for the other or anything like that; he says we compose our lives according to the laws of beauty, establishing that as the fundamental principle out of which the other flows of our lives emerge in turn. Our lives are first and foremost constructed on aesthetic principles, and the patterns we develop reflect laws that go beyond any subjective response to the world.

If existence is fundamentally aesthetic, though, one must ask why humans have resisted this knowledge for so long. After all, if Kundera is forced to assert that he will agree that coincidences are "novelistic" only as long as we do not interpret "novelistic" to mean "fictive," "fabricated" or "untrue to life," we must obviously have a heritage that suggests otherwise. We are normally inclined to do precisely what Kundera suspects: we will look at the coincidences of Tereza's and Tomas's life and belittle them because of their arbitrariness. Their lives look too contrived, we think, for in reality people don't fall in or out of love on the basis of such minor things as the number six or the music playing on the radio. Actually, we probably do know that people fall in love on the basis of such things, but we go along with Aristotle, who preferred his fictions to have probable improbabilities rather than improbable probabilities. And it is precisely that distinction which Kundera is attacking in his novel through the coincidences on which it is based.

Kundera is something of an experimental novelist in the sense that *The Unbearable Lightness of Being* is reflexive and regularly reminds us that it is a fiction, but as we have just seen, this distinction means something to Kundera that it doesn't ordinarily mean to us. If he has asserted that in some fundamental ways our very lives are fictional, if not in the way we think, it follows in turn that fictions are in some ways as real as our lives are, if not in the way we think. If an American writer like John Barth can humorously exploit the divide between fiction and life that engenders paralyzing self-consciousness because of one's awareness of how fictional (hence unreal) one's life really is in some respects and how real (hence fictional) one's fictions have become, Kundera locates the unreality of fictions elsewhere and is not concerned that his "unreal" characters might have nothing to do with the "reality" of our lives.

The characters are "unreal," to be sure. We are reminded of that again and again, most specifically with Tomas, who, we are told, was born of an image and of the saying "Einmal ist keinmal." Yet in spite of this "unreal" birth, Tomas's "life" in the novel takes on as much "reality," that is, "plausibility" and "richness" and "representational accuracy," as any character in a more traditional novel. Kundera does not call attention to the fictional nature of Tomas and Tereza to make us suspicious of the "reality" of their lives any more than he wants us to question in turn the fictionality of our own lives, at least when it comes to the compositions we create on the basis of the laws of beauty. Kundera is denying the value of the distinction "fictive, unreal" as it applies to both novels and lives, at least as it has developed over the past few hundred years.

The border between real and unreal is not something to be demarcated so easily by distinctions between "literature" and "life," and if there are useful and necessary discriminations to be made between the two, they certainly get lost in the endless babble about the unreality of our artificial linguistic and cultural artifacts and the artificiality of the lives we build on the basis of the constructs our culture presents us with. The crucial markers to be established disappear in this chaffering, Kundera would have us think, and we need therefore to return to a consideration of the notion that our lives are first and foremost aesthetic in nature, that we compose our lives according to the laws of beauty.

We compose our lives according to the laws of beauty, but.... There has to be a but in this utterance somewhere, for otherwise we would not have gotten into the trap that suggests "fiction" means "unreal." In some respects this too may only be a coincidence of our culture, but it is a coincidence we have built into a major motif by now, and if we did so, there must be a but that follows after the assertion that we compose our lives according to the laws of beauty. In *The Unbearable Lightness of Being*, that but is to be found in Kundera's discussion of kitsch, that phenomenon that truly does intersect the realm of the fictive and the unreal. And in his essayistic fashion, Kundera is quite straightforward in his exposition of our commitment to kitsch:

> Behind all the European faiths, religious and political, we find the first chapter of Genesis, which tells us that the world was created properly, that human existence is good, and that we are

therefore entitled to multiply. Let us call this basic faith a categorical agreement with being.

The fact that until recently the word "shit" appeared in print as s— has nothing to do with moral considerations. You can't claim that shit is immoral, after all! The objection to shit is a metaphysical one. The daily defecation session is daily proof of the unacceptability of Creation. Either/or: either shit is acceptable (in which case don't lock yourself in the bathroom!) or we are created in an unacceptable manner.

It follows, then, that the aesthetic ideal of the categorical agreement with being is a world in which shit is denied and everyone acts as though it did not exist. This aesthetic ideal is called kitsch.

"Kitsch" is a German word born in the middle of the sentimental nineteenth century, and from German it entered all Western languages. Repeated use, however, has obliterated its original metaphysical meaning: kitsch is the absolute denial of shit, in both the literal and the figurative senses of the word; kitsch excludes everything from its purview which is essentially unacceptable in human existence.

If Kundera's assertions about the place of the laws of beauty in our lives are in striking contrast to our own vision of things, that is because we have adopted a different aesthetic framework in order to convince ourselves that we have a categorical agreement with being. Inasmuch as we are unable to face certain aspects of our existence, expressed here by Kundera under the rubric of "shit," the only way we can bring ourselves to declare the creation good is to live in "a world in which shit is denied and everyone acts as though it did not exist." This is the world of kitsch.

Kitsch "excludes everything from its purview which is essentially un-acceptable in human existence," which means that it is an aesthetic based on unreal depictions of the way things are in order to establish a vision in which the world seems at least potentially a pleasing place to us. This view of the aesthetic, of course, is the one best expressed in Nietzsche's famous phrase that "We possess art lest we perish of the truth," and at base such a sentiment reflects a refusal to accept the nature of things at any level. More pertinently still, Kundera elaborates on the nature of the "shit" we deny when he tells us that "kitsch is a folding screen set up to curtain off death." In some respects "the daily defecation session" is no more than a reminder of our bodily natures and hence a demonstration of our mortality, that against which we so strenuously fight. So our world is based on the Bible and on Genesis, on the declaration of the world as essentially good, yet we don't really find it to be so and thus establish an aesthetic of denial rather than acceptance.

It is worth remembering that in contrast to the more famous statement quoted above, Nietzsche was finally devoted to a contrary thesis, one based on "Saying Yes to life even in its strangest and hardest problems," and this is certainly the sentiment of Kundera as well. Likewise, we need to recognize that although Kundera does finally associate kitsch with a fear of death, he begins with "shit," and not only because it is a more graphic depiction of our distaste for life but rather because it reflects something deeper than mere anxiety in the face of death: it manifests our shame. If Genesis asserts that the world is good and urges us to accede to this categorical agreement with being, it also makes clear that the first thing that Adam and Eve feel after they eat the apple is shame. Indeed, as a description of their prelapsarian state we are told in Genesis 2:25, "And they were both naked, the man and his wife, and were not ashamed," a statement suggesting that the distinguishing feature of life after the fall is shame. "Shit" symbolizes that shame, and the consequent revulsion at being human—and the inevitable denial of the categorical agreement with being—that the aesthetic of the West has been based on as far back as Plato's Republic.

The Unbearable Lightness of Being, then, establishes two kinds of aesthetic, the traditional one of kitsch, that aesthetic which begins by removing from our purview everything we find unpalatable about the world, and that aesthetic which is based on the attempt to say Yes to life even in its most difficult problems. Both conceptions of beauty are finally based on the essential relationship between beauty and shame, but the one begins by repressing that knowledge while the other embraces it as a necessary aspect of the overall whole. The one creates fictions that are deliberately "unreal," artifacts that are constructed in order to keep us from seeing what is real, and the other creates fictions that, while "artificial," nevertheless approach both the real and a categorical agreement with being.

The laws of beauty operate within both of these visions of the aesthetic, though one is more aware of the fact that the laws of beauty determine the motifs of one's life in the Kunderian perspective, and that is precisely the problem, for when the laws of beauty lose their essential connection to that which we construe as the shameful elements of life, they become disengaged from that which would be a sufficient measure of their "reality." If the real has been put out of play from the outset in the denial of shit, there is no way that the truth value of the aesthetic can be measured, for it has no linkage to the real in the first place. The only way to determine its reality quotient is to look for that which it represses, for when that is found, the aesthetic can be seen as one that is based on kitsch. Likewise, a life that is based on the laws of beauty and on a denial of shit at the same time will inevitably become an unreal life, one that establishes its sense of reality on the basis of kitsch.

If these two kinds of aesthetic were only relevant to the productions of the artistic world, the problem of shit and kitsch would be a relatively meaningless one; they would simply be the standard through which one could establish the validity of a work of art. The problem is that our vision of beauty is not restricted to such a localized environment. Kundera has already told us: "Behind all the European faiths, religious and political, we find the first chapter of Genesis, which tells us that the world was created properly, that human existence is good," and if we don't believe this to be the case, the religious and political faiths through which we construct our societies will reflect our refusal to agree with the conditions of being as they are established. This in turn means that our faiths will be based on an aesthetic of kitsch rather than on one that seriously seeks to address the shameful aspects of life: "Kitsch is the aesthetic ideal of all politicians and all political parties and movements." In this respect, the fictions with the highest unreality quotient are inevitably political, and they are so because the political system always appeals to our tendencies to want to deny that which is shameful.

Political kitsch is so dangerous because of the mechanisms through which it asserts its power. This is most obviously the case in the realm of what Kundera calls "totalitarian kitsch" because in such a world "everything that infringes on kitsch must be banished for life: every display of individualism (because a deviation from the collective is a spit in the eye of the smiling brotherhood); every doubt (because anyone who starts doubting details will end by doubting life itself); all irony (because in the realm of kitsch everything must be taken quite seriously)." And whereas we live in more or less pluralistic societies and thus in some respects manage to escape totalitarian kitsch, it is still the case that all political parties and movements depend on kitsch, and life is increasingly overwhelmed by the notion that society is nothing but political parties and movements.

The aesthetic of political kitsch is so dangerous precisely because it seems to saturate virtually every domain in the present world, from the domestic scene to the political movements we all recognize on the evening news. More importantly, the repression of shame that kitsch requires inevitably leads to problems of resentment and the need for victims when the world regularly turns out not to conform to the images of it that one's kitsch presents one with. Kundera gives us examples of the local expression of these problems throughout the novel. In Tereza's case, the embodiment of totalitarian kitsch is her mother, a woman who is determined to find someone to blame for a life gone wrong: "When [Tereza's mother] realized she had lost everything, she initiated a search for the culprit. Anyone would do: her first husband, manly and unloved, who had failed to heed her whispered warning; her second husband, unmanly and much loved, who had dragged her away from Prague to a small town and kept her in a state of permanent jealousy by going through one woman after another. But she was powerless against either. The only person who belonged to her and had no means of escape, the hostage who could do penance for all the culprits, was Tereza." Resentful over the outcome of her life, the product largely of her own choices and the aging process in general, Tereza's mother needs someone to blame for the unfortunate way things have gone and can find only Tereza for a victim. It doesn't matter that the mother's fate is not the fault of the daughter; what matters is that the mother herself find a way of placing the blame for the inevitabilities of her own life onto somebody else.

Curiously, though, Tereza's mother makes another gesture as well, one that would seem to deny the world of kitsch rather than uphold it: "Tereza's mother blew her nose noisily, talked to people in public about her sex life, and enjoyed demonstrating her false teeth. She was remarkably skillful at loosening them with her tongue, and in the midst of a broad smile would cause the uppers to drop down over the lowers in such a way as to give her face a sinister expression." Far from feeling shame in the face of her body and its decaying presence, the mother seems to revel in the most shameless of behavior and even ridicules Tereza when she tries to run from such actions. Rather than reflecting an acceptance of her lot, though, "Her behavior was but a single grand gesture, a casting off of youth and beauty. In the days when she had nine suitors kneeling round her in a circle, she guarded her nakedness apprehensively, as though trying to express the value of her body in terms of the modesty she accorded to it. Now she had not only lost that modesty, she had radically broken with it, ceremoniously using her new immodesty to draw a dividing line through her life and proclaim that youth and beauty were overrated and worthless."

These are hardly the acts of an individual who has put kitsch behind her; Tereza's mother has merely erected her own form of kitsch in order to deny her relationship to death and decay and to attempt to drag others down with her into a utopian community of non-difference: "Tereza's mother demanded justice. She wanted to see the culprit penalized. That is why she insisted her daughter remain with her in the world of immodesty, where youth and beauty mean nothing, where the world is nothing but a vast concentration camp of bodies, one like the next, with souls invisible." If all political images of kitsch are based on the ideal of a universal brotherhood— as Kundera phrases it, "The brotherhood of man on earth will be possible only on a base of kitsch"—Tereza's mother makes use of the same kitsch here, simply arriving at the universal brotherhood by a more ruthless way of stripping away the differences among people.

Tereza's mother is a terrorist, a totalitarian who seeks to impose her own kitschy image of reality onto others out of resentment and denial of who she herself really is, and in this she resembles all too much a great many political movements based on resentment and denial as well. Kundera provides an example from his own country to flesh out the seriousness of the problem:

> The first years following the Russian invasion could not yet be characterized as a reign of terror. Because practically no one in the entire nation agreed with the occupation regime, the Russians had to ferret out the few exceptions and push them into power. But where could they look? All faith in Communism and love for Russia was dead. So they sought people who wished to get back at life for something, people with revenge on the brain. Then they had to focus, cultivate, and maintain those people's aggressiveness, give them a temporary substitute to practice on. The substitute they lit upon was animals.

All at once the papers started coming out with cycles of features and organized letters-to-the-editor campaigns demanding, for example, the extermination of all pigeons within city limits. And the pigeons would be exterminated. But the major drive was directed against dogs. People were still disconsolate over the catastrophe of the occupation, but radio, television, and the press went on and on about dogs: how they soil our streets and parks, endanger our children's health, fulfill no useful function, yet must be fed.... Only after a year did the accumulated malice (which until then had been vented, for the sake of training, on animals) find its true goal: people. People started being removed from their jobs, arrested, put on trial. At last the animals could breathe freely.

If the occupying forces are to be able to maintain the fiction that the Russian invasion saved Czechoslovakia from certain ruin, someone must be blamed for the horrors the people had to go through. Moving from pigeons to dogs to people who are presumably inimical to the regime allows the Czech people to accommodate themselves to the victims they need, yet cannot admit to. After all, those who come to be victimized aren't really responsible for the fate of the nation, but, as with Tereza's mother, when one cannot fight back against those who are truly responsible—in this case the Russians—one must find someone else to blame or else seemingly die of shame.

In turn it is not an accident that the regime uses shame as its most masterful weapon, tape-recording conversations among the dissidents in order to discredit them by revealing their all-too-human pettinesses, by coercing individuals like Tomas into silence by way of demands for letters that explain their mistaken opposition to the occupying forces, and by making full use of the normal human tendency to buckle under in order to save one's own position in life. Tomas is forced to confront precisely this kind of shame and recognize its dual nature:

> Tomas was considered the best surgeon in the hospital. Rumor had it that the chief surgeon, who was getting on towards retirement age, would soon ask him to take over. When that rumor was supplemented by the rumor that the authorities had requested a statement of self-criticism from him, no one doubted he would comply.

That was the first thing that struck him: although he had never given people cause to doubt his integrity, they were ready to bet on his dishonesty rather than on his virtue.

The second thing that struck him was their reaction to the position they attributed to him. I might divide it into two basic types:

> The first type of reaction came from people who themselves (they or their intimates) had retracted something, who had themselves been forced to make public peace with the occupation regime or were prepared to do so (unwillingly, of course—no one wanted to do it)....

> The second type of reaction came from people who themselves (they or their intimates) had been persecuted, who had refused to compromise with the occupation powers or were convinced they would refuse to compromise (to sign a statement) even though no one requested it of them....

And suddenly Tomas grasped a strange fact: everyone was smiling at him, everyone wanted him to write the retraction; it would make everyone happy! The people with the first type of reaction would be happy because by inflating cowardice, he would make their actions seem commonplace and thereby give them back their lost honor. The people with the second type of reaction, who had come to consider their honor a special privilege never to be yielded, nurtured a secret love for the cowards, for without them their courage would soon erode into a trivial, monotonous grind admired by no one.

Both those who have been shamed and those who have had to demonstrate (or think they would demonstrate) courage want Tomas to sign a retraction in order to keep their fictions about themselves more comfortably in place. Those who are already shamed will be able to feel that their act was a normal one simply because Tomas, a man of considerable integrity, gave way under the force of the pressure too, and those who have resisted the pressures need to keep their grandiose vision of their courageous acts in place through repeated acts of humiliation on the part of others. Either way, shame is avoided as an essential aspect of the human condition, and either way the kitsch of the world increases.

What Kundera has given us, then, is a novel in which the characters explore the relationship between the aesthetic possibilities of the human condition and their connection to the political world of which they are also always a part. The book is based on the assumption that we invariably compose our lives according to the laws of beauty, but it also shows that those laws of beauty can move in two directions, in accord with the conventions of kitsch that dominate our social and political lives through their perpetual denial of the shit of life and the shame that is an inevitable part of it, or in line with an aesthetic that assumes a necessary relationship to the shame that came about in the moment that Adam and Eve ate the apple and that will never disappear from human existence. The latter vision is admittedly an "impure" one precisely to the extent that, like *The Unbearable Lightness of Being*, it reflects the ways in which the shit and the beauty of life are intermingled, but it is also an aesthetic that is devoted to the depiction of what is rather than to a repression of that which we should prefer to avoid in this world. And inasmuch as the novel demonstrates again and again the pernicious effects of a sociopolitical system that is based on the illusions of kitsch, the greater value of the impure form of beauty that Kundera presents us with is made manifest throughout the novel.

The direction of Kundera's aesthetic is reflected in his remarks on the value of heaviness, a commentary that embraces both the weighty decision of Beethoven's "Es muss sein" and the heavy burdens that Nietzsche envisioned through his conceptions of the eternal return and the overman. As the appropriate measure of our relation to heaviness, Kundera calls us to account for the relationship we have established with the animals, a relationship that is totally scandalous in all too many respects. This relationship too derives from our understanding of the first books of Genesis, so it is only fitting that Kundera should return there for his elaboration of our treatment of animals:

The very beginning of Genesis tells us that God created man in order to give him dominion over fish and fowl and all creatures. Of course, Genesis was written by a man, not a horse. There is no certainty that God actually did grant man dominion over other creatures. What seems more likely, in fact, is that man invented God to sanctify the dominion that he had usurped for himself over the cow and the horse. Yes, the right to kill a deer or a cow is the only thing all of mankind can agree upon, even during the bloodiest of wars.

If we asserted dominion over the other animals on the planet for ourselves and invented a God to justify that hubristic act, we know now that our reasons for doing so concerned our need for hierarchical priority, our desire to escape from the shame that would quickly follow in the Bible and from which we ourselves would never be able to escape. To one who is self-conscious, the killing of another animal has to be the most shameful of acts, far more horrifying than the mere recognition of one's own bodily nature and private parts. The endless parade of sacrifice that surrounds the killing of herds for food and the like testifies to our great need to escape from this shame and our thorough inability ever to do so.

But we tried, and when the dominion that the Bible gave to us was not sufficient to help us overcome our shame, we worked on other strategies, reflected most pertinently in Descartes and his attitude toward the animal world:

Even though Genesis says that God gave man dominion over all animals, we can also construe it to mean that He merely entrusted them to man's care. Man was not the planet's master, merely its administrator, and therefore eventually responsible for his administration.

Descartes took a decisive step forward: he made man "maître et propriétaire de la nature." And surely there is a deep connection between that step and the fact that he was also the one who point-blank denied animals a soul. Man is master and proprietor, says Descartes, whereas the beast is merely an automaton, an animated machine, a machine animata.

In order finally to escape from the degradation involved in our own bodily condition and that which stemmed from it—the need to devour other species—we had to take one more step and deny that animals had souls, thereby turning them into mere "automatons" that could be dispensed with as we saw fit, surely the way we continue to view them to this very day. In order, that is, to escape from our own degradation, we had to degrade completely all the rest of the species on the planet, the equivalent mode within the animal kingdom that we already saw at work in the political regimes represented by Tereza's mother and the occupying forces within Czechoslovakia.

For Kundera the degradation of animals reflects the larger human shame put on display throughout the novel: "True human goodness, in all its purity and freedom, can come to the fore only when its recipient has no power. Mankind's true moral test, its fundamental test (which lies deeply buried from view), consists of its attitude towards those who are at its mercy: animals. And in this respect mankind has suffered a fundamental debacle, a debacle so fundamental that all others stem from it." The kitsch through which we have framed our world—that sociopolitical aesthetic that is nothing more than "a folding screen set up to curtain off death"—has repeatedly attempted to escape from the scandal of its own hypocrisy, yet our need to deny our position in the world has prompted us again and again to degrade ourselves still further in the guise of a higher and purer vision to be found in the kitsch we so desperately want to believe in. There can be no doubt that we have devastated the species on the planet as a result of these urges, and thus one can only conclude that the aesthetic vision upon which our sense of the world has been based has been a complete failure and has shown itself to be morally bankrupt at the core.

The alternative aesthetic imagined by Kundera reflects a break with this tradition even as it acknowledges the chief originator of that break: Nietzsche. Kundera reflects on the moment when Nietzsche's madness overtook him and relates it to the human relationship with animals in order to establish the full difference between the Nietzschean view of things and the kitsch to which it was opposed:

> Seeing a horse and a coachman beating it with a whip, Nietzsche went up to the horse and, before the coachman's very eyes, put his arms around the horse's neck and burst into tears.

That took place in 1889, when Nietzsche, too, had removed himself from the world of people. In other words, it was at the time when his mental illness had just erupted. But for that very reason I feel his gesture has broad implications: Nietzsche was trying to apologize to the horse for Descartes. His lunacy (that is, his final break with mankind) began at the very moment he burst into tears over the horse.

And that is the Nietzsche I love, just as I love Tereza with the mortally ill dog resting his head in her lap. I see them one next to the other: both stepping down from the road along which mankind, "the master and proprietor of nature," marches onward.

Our tendency may be to want to quibble with this particular interpretation of the onset of Nietzsche's madness, arguing that Kundera is making far too much of it by suggesting that at this moment Nietzsche both apologizes to the horse for Descartes and steps down from the road on which our civilization continues to march, but given the full weight of existence and the necessary acceptance of it that Nietzsche was devoted to trying to embrace and affirm, there is every reason to think that this is not merely a "poetic"—and hence "fictive" and "unreal"—rendition of the stakes of this touching action on Nietzsche's part.

Like Kundera, Nietzsche was committed to a fundamentally aesthetic view of human existence, one that was both based on the laws of beauty and established through those laws the richness of life in the midst of its most shameful aspects, and if it took Kundera to recognize that the best measure of this new aesthetic was to be found in our relationship to the rest of the animals on the planet, he would be the first to admit that this insight is to be found at the very center of Nietzsche's work and is best represented by his final break with mankind over the shameless treatment of an animal that should not have had to bear our own shame for all these millennia. And if the image of Nietzsche in his madness hugging the horse is a most sobering gauge of the distance between an aesthetic of kitsch and one that embraces life in all of its beauty and shame, it should not deter us from questioning with continuing persistence another possible road for our own species to march on, nor should it keep us from realizing the degree to which our lives continue to be composed according to the laws of beauty even when we least expect it.

MICHAEL CARROLL

The Cyclic Form of Laughable Loves

The fiction of Milan Kundera has inspired an avalanche of critical
attention in recent years; in fact, as we come to realize the importance of his
work, Kundera studies are becoming, as this volume evidences, something of
a "growth industry." The works that have attracted the greatest critical
attention are his most recent (and most fully realized) offerings: *The Book of
Laughter and Forgetting* and *The Unbearable Lightness of Being*. However, in
order to understand Kundera's work as a whole, we must turn back to his
earliest fiction. We must do so, first of all and most obviously, because there
is a thematic nexus that links all of the works of any given writer's oeuvre;
naturally, we find that these works as a whole are characterized by certain (we
might say "Kunderan") preoccupations. Second, we must do so in order to
understand the aesthetic trajectory of his career, for these works not only
represent a continuation of the traditional function of prose fiction as
thematic exploration through what Kundera (in *Art of the Novel*) refers to as
nondidactic discourse: they also continue another tradition, that of formal
complexity and experimentation—the tradition of, to name a few, Conrad,
Kafka, and Nabokov. Kundera's aesthetic trajectory is best understood by
turning to his very first work as a fiction writer, *Laughable Loves*, a work
which serves as the aesthetic prototype for *The Book of Laughter and
Forgetting* and to some extent *The Unbearable Lightness of Being*.

From *Milan Kundera and the Art of Fiction*, edited by Aron Aji, Garland Publishing Inc., 1992.
Reprinted in Short Story Criticism, Vol. 24. © 1992 by Routledge, Inc.

Unfortunately, the importance of this early work is generally overlooked; this is in part due to the fact that until quite recently a definitive English-language edition has not been available.

Laughable Loves has, for a contemporary work, a rather involved publication history. As Kundera himself remarked in an interview with Lois Oppenheim [in *Review of Contemporary Fiction*, 2 (1989)], his first short story "I, Sad God" (1959), marks the end of his career as a poet and playwright and the beginning of his career as a fiction writer. In 1963, this story and two others ("My Nurse Above All Others" and "Nobody Will Laugh") were published (by Cekoslovensky Spisovateil, the Czech state publishing organ) in a single volume, entitled Smesne Lasky [*Laughable Loves*]. In 1965, a Second Book of *Laughable Loves* was published: it included "The Golden Apple of Eternal Desire," "The Herald," and perhaps the most renowned Kundera story, "The Hitchiking Game." In 1968, a Third Book of *Laughable Loves* was published; it included "Let the Old Dead Make Room for the Young Dead," "Symposium," "Edward and God," and "Doctor Havel After Ten Years."

The three separate books were published for the first time as a single volume in 1970— the last book by Kundera to be published in his native land (although with the Czech revolution of November 1989, there can be no doubt that Kundera's works will once again be available in his own country). In this edition, Kundera eliminated two of the stories ("My Nurse Above All Others" and "The Herald") but otherwise retained the same order and the tripartite structure, which is indicated in this volume by upper case Roman numerals and a blank page between each volume.

Also in 1970, Gallimard Publishers released a first French edition of Risibles Amours. Kundera decided to drop yet another story ("I, Sad God"), leaving seven of the original ten. For the first French edition Kundera also eliminated the tripartite division indicated by the Roman numerals and inverted the ordering of the last two pairs of stories, forming what would be the final, intended arrangement:

Nobody Will Laugh

The Golden Apple of Eternal Desire

The Hitchhiking Game

Symposium

Let the Old Dead Make Room for the Young Dead

Doctor Havel After Ten Years

Edward and God

The French edition was followed by Polish and Italian editions, and in 1974, the first English-language edition (Knopf). However, this first English edition (as Kundera points out in an Poznamka autora [Author's Note] which accompanies the 1981 Czech-language edition published in Toronto) presents the stories in an arbitrary order. During this period just before his emigration, Kundera had a difficult time managing his affairs. The arrangement for the English edition was done, as he points out, without his knowledge, and he was not happy with it. The first English] edition obscures the relationship between *Laughable Loves* and the work for which it served as a prototype, *The Book of Laughter and Forgetting*. This is no small matter, for Kundera's fiction, like that of James Joyce, is characterized by an almost obsessive concern for the architectonics of narrative form. To read the stories of *Laughable Loves* in random order is no more critically acceptable than it would be to read Joyce's *Dubliners* in like fashion. In any case, this first English edition was reprinted for the first time by Penguin in 1975 and then reprinted (according to the publishing information in the revised edition of the text) nine times between 1980 and 1988.

In 1979, Gatlimard provided Kundera with the opportunity to revise, resulting in a definitive French edition. The ordering of the stories was the same as that of the 1970 French edition, but Kundera made a number of relatively minor textual changes. In 1981, the firm 88 Publishers (located in Toronto) published a definitive Czech edition, and in 1987, Penguin published the first definitive English-language edition, which followed the ordering of stories indicated in the Gallimard.

When read in its intended arrangement, *Laughable Loves* is a work with a totalizing form. This was apparent even before the work was at last completed. After the second volume of *Laughable Loves* was published, a number of Czech reviewers pointed in one way or another to the volumes' common thematic center. Juri Opelik, for instance, noted [in a review in Listy 15 (1969)] that the stories use the theme of sexuality to examine problems of memory. Another Czech critic, Milan Blahynka, noted [in a review in Pinmen 1 (1967)] that the first two volumes of *Laughable Loves* can be seen as having an overall dialectic pattern. And in an article on Kundera published in 1975, Robert Porter extends Blahynka's notion of a dialectical pattern in the cycle to include all three volumes. According to Porter, the first volume of stories center on characters who fail in their efforts to control the lives of others, while the second volume demonstrates that people are not even capable of controlling their own lives, for "a new dimension may suddenly emerge, a game may become too real, a joke become a tragedy." In the third volume, Porter sees a synthesis: having shown that man cannot control the lives of others or, for that matter, his own, man must now "come to terms with the world and with what freedom he has" ("Freedom Is My Love," *Index on Censorship* 4, No. 4, 1975). In very schematic terms, then, Blahynka and Porter correctly identify the thematic unity and complex interplay of parts in this work.

The arrangement, the unity, and the interplay of discrete narrative units in *Laughable Loves* is not, of course, unique. Forrest L. Ingram, in a ground-breaking study entitled "Representative Short Story Cycles of the Twentieth Century: Studies in a Literary Genre," brought critical attention to bear on a number of notable cycles such as *Dubliners*, *The Hunger Artist*, and Steinbeck's *The Pastures of Heaven*. Ingram defines the story cycle as a "set of stories linked to each other in such a way as to maintain a balance between the individuality of each of the stories and the larger unit." An important element of this fundamental scheme is a dynamic tension between the independence and the inter-dependence of the constituent parts—a structural ambiguity. Every story cycle, says Ingram, is characterized by a "double tendency of asserting the individuality of its components" while simultaneously asserting "the bonds of unity which make the many into a single whole." The individual units of the cycle are discrete in that they have their own beginnings, middles, and ends, and that they can be read as complete works in and of themselves—they can stand up on their own without the contextual support of the cycle. The totality of the cycle, on the other hand, results from what Ingram calls the "dynamic patterns of recurrence and development."

The patterns of recurrence may be of several varieties; for example, a thematic axis—in the case of *Dubliners*, the "paralysis" of Irish culture. Certain characters or character types may also provide a repetitive pattern, as with Nick Adams in Hemingway's *In Our Times*, who, as Susan Garland Mann notes in her study of this genre, serves as the work's "most explicit unifying device." The pattern of development, on the other hand, may assume the same forms but in a way that creates a linear trajectory and thus a kind of mega-narrative for the cycle: in *Dubliners* the characters become progressively older as one moves through the cycle; more significantly, as Brewster Ghiselin observes [in "The Unity of *Dubliners*," Accent, Spring, 1956], there is a discernible "movement of the human soul, in desire of life, through various conditions." And in Faulkner's *The Unvanquished* Ingram observes a "logically sequential development of action" as one moves from story to story. The twin patterns of recurrence and development, then, account for a cycle's unity, and these patterns are set in opposition to the independence, the sense of self-containedness and closure, of each of the constituent narrative units. It should be noted that none of this need be symmetrical—some stories in a cycle may be fiercely independent, even to the point of seeming out of place. Other stories may form subsets, a strategy that is an important part of Kundera's two cyclic works: the stories "Symposium" and "Dr. Havel After Twenty Years" establish the only instance of narrative continuity (in the usual sense) in *Laughable Loves*; this is likewise true of Parts Four and Six of *The Book of Laughter and Forgetting*. In this instance, a particular bonding of stories gives the work added coherence to stabilize, as it were, the contrasting pull of disunity. On the other hand, as Gerald Kennedy points out in his study of the short story cycle [in "Towards a Poetics of the Short Story Cycle," *Journal of the Short Story in English* 11 (1988)], clusters of stories within a collection "may give special attention to a particular idea; in effect, such combinations form a sequence within a sequence." This is precisely what Maria Banerjee observes in her recent essay on a pair of stories in *Laughable Loves*. She notes that in "The Golden Apple of Eternal Desire," and "Doctor Havel After Twenty Years," Kundera makes explicit use of the Don Juan myth ["The Impossible Don Juan," *Review of Contemporary Fiction*] 2 (1989)]. In the former story, we find a variation on that "mythical pair of sexual adventures, Don Juan and is servant" and in the latter, the young editor is reminiscent of Don Juan's servant while Havel's wife reminds us of the pursuing spouse, Elvira.

Another important aspect of Ingram's theory is the notion of a "spectrum" of story cycles, which in turn suggests three sub-genres: the composed, the arranged, and the completed cycle. The composed cycle is one which the author "had conceived as a whole from the time he wrote its first story," and as such the author composes his work according to the demands of a "master plan." The arranged cycle is at the other end of the spectrum, consisting of stories "which an author or editor-author has brought together to illuminate or comment upon one another by juxtaposition or association," and they are obviously the "loosest" of story cycles. The third sub-genre that Ingram describes is the "completed" cycle, which consists of stories that are neither strictly composed nor arranged. They may have begun as independent dissociated stories. But soon their author became conscious of unifying strands which he may have, even subconsciously, woven into the action of the stories. Consciously, then, he completed the unifying task which he may have subconsciously begun.

Two notable examples of the third type, the completed cycle, are found in Kafka's *Ein Hungerkunstler* and Eudora Welty's *The Golden Apples*. Although the stories of Kafka's cycle were written over a period of four years, and despite the fact that one of the four was previously published, it is also true that Kafka carefully selected the stories he wished to include in a single volume and that he firmly insisted that the stories be arranged in a particular way. Welty likewise had strong feelings about the arrangement of her story cycle, and her comments on the composing process in the case of cyclic form are revealing. "All this time in the back of my head," Welty says, "these connections had worked themselves out. I had just go get the clue, like a belated detective ..." (*Conversations with Eudora Welty*, edited by Peggy Whitman, 1984). Apparently, the cyclic mode of composition was ingrained in Kundera as an aesthetic practice before he even turned to fiction. Kundera's father was a noted music professor, and Kundera himself was a musician and composer during the first phase of his artistic career. In *Art of the Novel*, Kundera goes to impressive extremes to demonstrate that the architectonics of his literary works are derived from his musical ideas. In discussing one of his early compositions, he notes that it

> was almost a caricature preview of the architecture of my novels, whose future existence I didn't even faintly suspect at that time. That Composition for Four Instruments is divided—imagine!— into seven parts. As in my novels, the piece consists of parts that are very hererogenous in form.... That formal diversity is balanced by a very strong thematic unity: from start to finish, only two themes ... are elaborated.

These cyclic tendencies carried over to Kundera's first literary efforts: as Opelik notes, *Laughable Loves* bears considerable resemblance to Kundera's lyric cycle, *Monology*. In this respect, Kundera's literary career parallels that of two other notable writers: James Joyce's poem cycle, *Chamber Music*, is clearly a prelude to *Dubliners*; William Faulkner's *Visions of Spring Day* may likewise be viewed as a formal experiment that paved the way for *Go Down, Moses*. In this regard, all three writers may be said to possess what P. M. Kramer, in her work on cyclic form, has called a "cyclic habit of mind" [The Cyclical Method of Composition in Gottfried Keller's "Das Sinngedicht," 1939].

Given that Kundera wrote the stories of *Laughable Loves* over a ten-year period and that the final form of the work came to him in the process of composition, arrangement, and rearrangement, it seems clear that it may be regarded as (to use Ingram's "spectrum") a completed cycle, and that his experience in the creation of this work inevitably influenced the form of *The Book of Laughter and Forgetting*, a much more aesthetically ambitious and unified work—a composed cycle. As Kundera himself said in a 1983 interview, in the process of eliminating three of the original ten stories and arranging the final version, "the collection had become very coherent, foreshadowing the composition of *The Book of Laughter and Forgetting*" ("The Art of Fiction LXXXI," *Paris Review*, Summer, 1984). This makes it all the more apparent that to read the stories of *Laughable Loves* in random order would be to disregard the authorial intent and the aesthetic coherence of this work.

The question of response, important in the study of any literary form, is particularly important in the study of cyclic texts, for their generic nature is not signaled by any traditional code —and yet, they elicit in the reader, in the process of successive interpretive activities, a sense of their generic nature. They provide for a particular kind of literary experience. As Ingram points out, the stories of a cycle are connected in such a way that the "reader's experience of each is modified by his experience of others." Further, "while each story in a cycle may be relatively simple, the dynamic of the cycle itself often poses a major challenge to the critic.... Shifting internal relationships, of course, continually alter the originally perceived pattern of the whole cycle." In spite of this statement, however, Ingram's analyses of various story cycles do not attempt to reconstruct this dynamism: Ingram's " fundamental assumptions," as he puts it, are in keeping with the New Critical formalism of Cleanth Brooks. Thus, as Gerald Kennedy notes in a recent article on the "poetics" of story cycles, Ingram treats the "unity of those works as an intrinsic feature of the writing rather than as a function or product of his own reading." Nonetheless, Ingram is absolutely correct in pointing to the "challenge to the critic" which is entailed in such an endeavor. The challenge is that of tracing a hypothetic reading activity as it moves through the maze of textual connections.

What happens when we read, and more particularly, what happens when we read a cyclic text? The most satisfying answers, it seems to me, are to be found in phenomenology, particularly in Wolfgang Iser's adaption of Husserl's foundational concept, protension and retention:

> ... throughout the reading process there is a continual interplay between modified expectations and transformed memories. However, the text itself does not formulate expect-ations or their modification; nor does it specify how the

connectability of memories is to be implemented. This is the
province of the reader himself, and so here we have a first insight
into how the synthesizing activity of the reader enables the text
to be translated and transferred to his own mind. This process of
translation also shows upon the basic hermeneutic structure of
reading. Each sentence correlate contains what one might call a
hollow section, which looks forward to the next corrolate, and a
retrospective section, which answers the expectations of the
preceding sentence (now a part of the background). Thus every
moment of reading is a dialectic of protension and retention,
conveying a future horizon yet to be occupied, along with a past
(and continually fading) horizon already filled.... [*The Act of
Reading*, 1978]

In her essay on cyclic form, Agnes Goreben discusses a similar
phenomenon, although her grammatics are on the level of narratological
units rather than the sentence and are thus even more well-suited for our
purposes. She refers to this feature as the "network of cross-reference" in
cyclic texts. As she explains it, if a prior narrative unit of a given story cycle
contains, for instance, "an objectified simile, a situation, an attitude or value,"
and this given element reoccurs in a later narrative unit, then there is no
'vacuum' in the reader's mind where it tries to find its location, but it
'triggers' a field in it that has already been conditioned" ["The Syntactics of
Cycles of Short Stories," *Essays in Poetics*, 1 (1986)].

Regarding *Laughable Loves*, a good place to start is in the middle, for by
doing so we may trace several strands of the dialectic of retention. The title
of the third story, "The Hitchhiking Game," demonstrates how textual
structures such as sub-titles and prefaces may serve as a key to form and
meaning, for it announces that we shall most likely be presented with
characters who are game players, and with this a pro-conditioned field is
"triggered." That is, even by the second story of the cycle ("The Golden
Apple of Eternal Desire") a perceptible pattern of games, established in the
first story ("Nobody Will Laugh"), becomes evident. In the protagonists of
the first two stories, Klima and Martin respectively, we have the repetition of
a character type in that they are both deeply involved in "games" that are
hopelessly and pathologically out-of-control. In Klima's case the problem is
so severe that it is not so much that he is playing a joke as it is that he is being
played by a joke. He continues in his refusal to write a review of Zaturetsky's
article and thus embarks on a peculiar game of hiding from the man. His
motivation in this regard is complex: he enjoys Zaturetsky's adulation of him,

and as a result he has no desire to devastate the man by rejecting his mediocre review. More importantly, however, he is intimidated by Zaturetsky's strong will, and more importantly still, there is his love for the "game"—a game that turns the respected scholar into a child lost in a fantasy world. In his delight at having successfully eluded Zaturetsky through a series of ruses, Klima exclaims, "I longed to put on a bowler hat and stick on a beard. I felt like Sherlock Holmes or the invisible man ... I felt like a little boy." His game inevitably leads to his downfall—to the examining committee and dismissal (an institution and an act that are repeatedly portrayed in Kundera's fiction).

Martin's game is likewise compulsive and out of control, and, like Klima's, regressive in nature: womanizing is Martin's way of denying that he is getting old. As the narrator explains, Martin has "the most regular sort of marriage" and "above this reality (and simultaneous with it), Martin's youth continues, a restless, gay, and erring youth transformed into a mere game." In these two stories, then, the reader finds a repetition, the simultaneous presence of similarity and difference: the game played by Martin in "Golden Apple" is, first of all, an ironic inversion of the one played by Klima, for in Klima's game of lying and avoidance, it is he, Klima, who is the prey while Zaturetsky. is the pursuer; conversely, it is Martin who is the pursuer and women— women of all kinds—who are the prey. Furthermore, the reader's initial recognition of cyclicity informs an act of protension: the reader will be inclined to expect more of the same, and the ensuing narrative units will be read with the suspicion that recurrent themes, character types, and tropes may be lurking therein. Iser calls this the "the consistency building habit which underlies all comprehension." Thus, the observation of a thematic connection between the second and the first stories leads inexorably to other connections, leads to the filling of conceptual "gaps." The reader has begun to intuit the genre.

And thus, to return now to where we were—at the beginning of the third story, "The Hitchhiking Game"—the reader enters the story proconditioned by the game motif. The game played by the young man and his girl (the characters in this story are weirdly anonymous) is yet another kind of game: he pretends to be the type of man who uses women as mere instruments of pleasure, while she, at first coerced by the young man but later doing so of her own volition, plays the role of the freewheeling, lascivious woman. As different as this game is from those played in the previous two stories, there is yet an underlying similarity: Martin pretends to be a young man merrily going about the business of sowing his wild oats while he is in fact a middle-aged married man; Klima, the college professor, pretends to be a prankish schoolboy. It is furthermore noteworthy that the young man provides another example of the regressive personality type, for his desire to be the "heartless tough guy," we are told, is rooted in the "childish desires [which] withstand all the snares of the adult mind and often survive into ripe old age." Through this psychological profile, the underlying similarity between the regressive types—Klima, Martin, and the young man— merges quite unmistakably. And as in the case of the game played by Klima, the young couple's game of make-believe along with their lack of foresight soon gets out of control and leads to yet another downfall. For Klima, that downfall is the destruction of a career; for the couple in the present story, it is the destruction of a relationship. This game motif continues through a number of other stories in the cycle, in particular the "Havel stories," both of which revolve around cruel hoaxes.

At this stage of the cycle another thematic gestalt begins to emerge: the related notions of womanizing, eroticism, and sexual identity. The successive kinds of womanizing which become apparent as one moves through the cycle forms an ironic sequence: in the first story, we have a man (Zaturetsky) who is in no way a womanizer but who is nonetheless accused (by the playful Klima) of being one. In the second story, we have a skillful lady's man (Martin, who has gone so far as to create a bizarre kind of science of the activity, replete with its own jargon) who would be a full-blown womanizer were it not for his essential conventionality and his guilty regard for his wife. And in the third story, we have a young man who fantasizes about being a lewd, whoring tough-guy, a womanizer of the worst kind, while he is actually a typical young man in a typical monogamous relationship.

It is in the fourth story, "Symposium," in the character of Alzhbeta, that the reader finds thematic and imagistic elements which enable him to once again cast back through the text in order to form a larger constellation of meaning. When Alzhbeta performs a mock strip-tease for a rather uninterested group of doctors, the resultant image strongly echoes the young woman's strip-tease in "The Hitchhiking Game," a fact which points to the special power of mental imagery in the process of constructing text totality. And yet, even as the reader notes this similarity, there are also a number of discernible and significant differences. The young woman of the previous story has to assume the role of the whore in order to feel comfortable with her sexuality. Alzhbeta, on the other hand, is fully at ease with her body— indeed, her only problem seems to be getting someone to take notice of it, and thus she cries out "Look at me! I am alive anyhow!.... For the time being I am still alive!" This refrain clearly recalls the "pitiful tautology" of the young woman: "I am me, I am me ..." The ironic inversion (a trope repeatedly invoked as the spokes of the cycle come together), however, is that while Alzhbeta wants her sexuality to be noticed, the young woman wants her lover to forget her sexuality (manifested in her role as the whore) and recall her inner, personal identity.

The endings of narratives—cycles included—hold a position of particular importance in terms of the reading process. At the moment of textual closure, the process of protension has ceased, for there is no more text for the reader to anticipate. At this juncture the reader's attention becomes fully retentive, and the text becomes less a temporal and more a spacial entity: as Elaine Torgovnick notes, the text now "seems to pose before our eye to assume its geometry" [*Closure in the Novel*, 1981]. The activity which takes place at the point of closure, a point at which the reader looks back into the text with the desire to grasp its totality, is best described by Barbara Smith's term, "retrospective patterning" [*Poetic Closure*, 1968]. The term is apt, for it encapsulates the paradoxical combination of dynamism (retrospection is an activity, a mental process) and stasis (a pattern is a static entity). The patterns that congeal, to return to Ingram's theory, may either be linear or repetitive—what Ingram calls "patterns of development" and "patterns of recurrence" respectively. Furthermore, entirely new thematic configurations may be triggered by the activity. As Iser notes, a basic element of the reading process, is this succession of gestalt formations; furthermore, "each gestalt bears with it those possibilities which it has excluded but which may eventually invalidate it." Acts of memory and reinterpretation within the reading process, then, can allow for a conceptual realignment of text which had already been conceptualized. The parts of a cycle are indeed, as Ingram says, like the moving and shifting parts of a mobile.

Placing the reader at the end of the cycle—that is, at the seventh and final story, "Edward and God"—we can observe a number of ways in which the thematic gestalten which evolve during the process of moving through the cycle become "retrospectively patterned." To return to our discussion of the various female characters in the cycle, Chehachkova, the major female figure of the seventh story, is, at first, completely unlike any of the other female characters we have encountered thus far. She is, first and foremost, a dedicated Communist. But when she decides to confess her innermost beliefs, she reveals that she holds a transcendental view—albeit a kind of socialist transcendentalism. Chehachkova espouses a belief in something beyond the self—"man is not in this world for his own sake." At this point a linear pattern in terms of the representation of women in the cycle is revealed: as we have moved towards the end of the cycle, the female characters become progressively more inclined to make pronouncements as per the possibility of transcending mortality. Consider the woman in the fifth story, "Let the Old Dead Make Room for the Young Dead," who sees her son as an extension of her life and who believes that a man's accomplishments transend his physical being. Consider also Doctor Frantishka (from the sixth story, "Dr. Havel After Twenty Years"), who makes similar proclamations to her young lover. Given this trend, it seems with the title "Edward and God" that perhaps we have been inevitably led to the transcendent word and concept par excellence. And indeed, the story ends with Edward in a church. And though the narrator notes that the story does not end with "so ostentatious a paradox" as Edward's religious conversion, he does long for the God who does not exist.

Chehachkova is furthermore related to other female characters in the text in that she too will strip before the examining eye of the male. She is thus the final link in a chain of women (enchained women) who are put time and again in this (usually compromising) position. And like the women in "The Hitchhiking Game" and "Symposium," she wants her partner to see not merely her appearance, but her inner essence, and thus her cry—"I am not a boring woman! That I am not"—is but another version of Alzhbeta's "Look at me ... I am alive" and the young woman's lament, "I am me!" Moreover, her male counterpart is much like the other male counterparts in that he finds a certain excitement in subjecting women to degradation. The scene in which Edward forces Chehachkova to kneel naked before him while reciting the Lord's Prayer clearly recalls the strip scene in "Hitchhiking Game," but with (yet another) ironic inversion: whereas the young man in the previous story got his thrills by making his lover act like a whore while doing a striptease, Edward wants Chehachkova to behave like a devout Christian (fitting, for she is indeed a Stalinist nun). In both cases the result is the same—degradation for the female, excitement for the male.

Thus, at this late juncture in the cycle yet another thematic gestalt emerges, a socio-sexual one triggered by the repeated female image—the "games" the various male characters play are often at the expense of women. This is most obviously the case in the Havel stories and "The Hitchhiking Game." However, upon reconsideration and a realignment of what Gereben calls "the network of cross-reference," it is true of other characters in the cycle as well: consider the way Professor Klima toys with Klara, offering her false promises of a better life. Or Martin, who thinks nothing of "registering" a woman, making a date, and then leaving her in the lurch, and thus Martin is another punishing womanizer. Or the male protagonist of "Let the Old Dead Make Room for the Young Dead," whose sexual desire "was mixed with the desire to debase" the woman from his past.

Of the various forms of closural patterns, the most relevant, of course, to the cycle is what Torgovnick, in her catalogue of closural activities, calls circularity, which occurs when the ending "clearly recalls the beginning in some way, perhaps in its language or in situation." In *Laughable Loves*, this occurs through character, for Chehachkova's male counterpart, Edward, is almost a re-en-actment of Professor Klima. Like Klima, Edward experiences an exhilarating moment of freedom when he does something he knows he shouldn't—in this case attending a Catholic Mass. In the church, Edward could not resist a "compelling desire" to kneel, to cross himself, in short, to "do something he'd never done before," and in so doing he feels "magnificently free." And like Klima, he is a teacher, one who is, moreover, under the scrutiny of those who doubt he is fit to teach. Edward's story is also one of persecution and that peculiar Stalinist institution, the examining committee. Finally, as in the case of Klima and other characters we have discussed, Edward finds that once one has started a game, it takes on a life of it own and sweeps one along with it, whether one wishes it to or not.

The more political nature of "Edward and God" (overt references to the death of Stalin, the revolutionary generation, and the polarized nature of Czech society after the revolution) along with the way it mirrors the first story of the cycle together set the stage for textual realignment and transformation. In the final story, the examination of political structures re-emerges, retentively reactivates similar material in the first unit of the cycle, and, as though illuminated by refracted light bouncing back and forth between the opening and closing units, the political ramifications (dormant in the reader's consciousness since Klima's ordeal with the examining committee) of the intervening units become emphasized.

Take "The Hitchhiking Game." The young man, as we have seen, is drawn towards the brutal results of his fantasy. But what lies behind the game? What is the motive? "The main road of [the young man's] life," we are told, "was drawn with implacable precision.... Even two weeks' vacation didn't give him a feeling of liberation and adventure; the gray shadow of precise planning lay even here." When he decides to take the road which leads to some place other than their all-too-planned vacation, it pushes the game "into a higher gear," but it also stands as a decisive move towards freedom, a break with the gloomy and monotonous "plannedness" of things. The girl's willingness to play the game and become the fantasy woman, the woman of "happy go lucky irresponsibility," is similar: "... she had quite a tiresome job ... and a sick mother. So she often felt tired.... She didn't have particularly good nerves or self-confidence and easily fell into a state of anxiety or fear."

An important part of their motive, then, is to escape the dismal limitations of their life. Once the reader comes to this realization, it can be connected with what he has read in other parts of the cycle, and this thematic gestalt absorbs other units of text. Thus, Martin's womanizing seemed at first to be largely a matter of trying to deny the aging process and the ineluctable forward march of time. But we will also remember that he is a married man with a job, and his erotic games must be cut short so that he can get home by the matrimonially-imposed deadline of 9:00 p.m. And so he too plays a game not only because of his regressive personality, but, at least in a limited sense, as a bid for freedom. Dr. Havel reveals similar motives when he rationalizes his rejection of a woman (a bizarre move for a confirmed womanizer). He first states that, given his predictable behavior, he should have slept with her: "All the statistics would have worked it out that way." And then he quickly adds that "perhaps for those very reasons, I don't take her. Perhaps I want to resist necessity. To trip up causality. To throw off the predictability of the world's course through the whimsicality of caprice." As Banerjee notes, Don Juans do what they do in order to escape "the dull anonymity of their social condition." Much the same is true of the male character of the fifth story ("Let the Old Dead Make Room for the Young Dead"), whose desire to recapture the past is the flip side of his reconciliation to his "not too exciting life ... and the monotonous rowdiness which surrounded him at work." Furthermore, Klima's game with Zaturetsky, a game which initially seemed to be a manifestation of a regressive personality, is now opened for re-conceptualization and can become part of a new thematic configuration, one based on a social rather than psychoanalytic model. After all, early in that story, after he had been more-or-less ordered to follow standard procedure and write a nasty letter to Zaturestsky trashing his work, Klima thinks to himself, "why should I have to be Mr. Zaturetsky's executioner?" Thus, Klima's game may also be seen as an attempt to break away from narrow organizational limits.

It is clear that these characters share similar motivations. They all seem, as Havel articulates it (speaking, as it were, on behalf of the other characters), to want to "derail life from its dreary predictability." Those games may thus be viewed as originating in a desire to break free from a rigid social order, and thus those game-players may be driven not only by psychopathological conditions, but also by their discontent with the social arena in which they play. They are trapped by routine, and the reader's recognition of this reinforces the deepening impression that the effects of social and political conditions on the individual is a central theme of this work.

This dynamic, in terms of response and closure, illustrates the operation of " retrospective patterning," which in this case encourages the emergence of a thematic gestalt that is political in nature: in the final conceptualization, when one lifts the photographic plate from the chemical bath, a portrait of a politically-oppressive society is seen to have developed. However mild, ironic, and subdued that portrait may be, it is nonetheless unmistakably there. It is important to note, however, that the characters of *Laughable Loves* are never more than dimly aware of their collective malady, and this very lack of awareness emerges as an important corollary of this thematic core. Character after character, one realizes in retrospect, is peculiarly blind to his own motivations and to where his actions lead. Certainly, Edward moves blindly towards disaster, as do the young man ("Hitchhiking Game") and Martin. This blindness is perhaps most apparent in the very first story, "Nobody Will Laugh." Klima himself puts it in no uncertain terms: "man passes," he says, "through the present with his eyes blindfolded.... Only later when the cloth is untied can he glance at the past and find out what he has experienced and what meaning it had." Which, it occurs to me, may be taken as an allegory for the reading process itself, particularly in regards to the dialectic of retention and closural activities. The reader must, if he wishes to pass through the text at all, proceed at least partially "blindfolded" with the understanding that meaning generally emerges in retrospect.

As with *Laughable Loves*, Kundera's later work, *The Book of Laughter and Forgetting*, may be described as having a cyclic form; a number of critics have commented upon this in terms that clearly resemble Ingram's definition. John Updike, for example, notes that the book is "more than a collection of seven stories yet certainly no novel" [*Hugging the Shore*, 1988]. In like fashion, Terry Eagleton points out that the "structural subversiveness" of this work "lies simply in the loose consciousness whereby they encompass different stories, sometimes to the point of appearing like a set of nouvelles within the same covers" ["Estrangement and Irony," *Salmagundi* 73 (1987)]. R. B. Gill, in an explicit comparison of *The Book* and *Dubliners*, suggests that it is best regarded not as a novel "in the usual sense, [but as] a series of parts, one could call then stories, each thematically related to the others, a series of variations on a theme" ["Bargaining in Good Faith: The Laughter of Vonnegut, Grass, and Kundera," in *Milan Kundera and the Art of Fiction*, ed. Aron Aji]. And as David Lodge notes in a statement that reveals the way in which the critic must inevitably deal with cycles, "the only way to deal, critically, with *The Book of Laughter and Forgetting* is to review its textual strategies in the order in which they are experienced by the reader" ["Milan

Kundera, and the Idea of the Author in Modern Criticism," *Critical Quarterly*, Spring-Summer, 1984].

For all their similarities, there are also significant differences between these two works. Perhaps the most important and innovative of those features is *The Book's* "poly-generic" character. The stories of *Laughable Loves* are, in and of themselves, short stories of a relatively conventional sort. By contrast, *The Book* is made up of seven Parts which in turn are fragmented in that they constitute a generic smorgasbord: informal essay (history, musicology, philosophy), the fantastic, and autobiography. As Herbert Eagle remarks [in "Genre and Paradigm in Milan Kundera's *The Book of Laughter and Forgetting*," in *Language and Literal Theory*, edited by Benjamin A. Stolz and others, 1984], Kundera is a writer whose mastery covers a number of widely divergent genres aside from fiction —poetry, the essay, and, in the Czech tradition, feuilletons. "In this diverse oeuvre," Eagle notes, there are persistent themes that, in *The Book*, Kundera explores in a format which allows him to write "in all of his favorite genres simultaneously.... "Thus, while *The Book* is certainly in cyclic form, it is not, to be precise, a short story cycle, and it thus exceeds its generic identity (perhaps it is more accurate to call it a "polygeneric cycle"). *The Book* also obviously differs from *Laughable Loves* in that it is peppered with statements which address the problems of fictional discourse, a genre which has come to be termed metafiction. As Charles Molesworth asserts [in "Kundera and *The Book*: The Unsaid and the Unsayable," in *Milan Kundera and the Art of Fiction*, ed. Aron Aji] "The Book, in addition to its thematic unity, has a structural unity that is achieved by its "concern with itself as a novel."

Furthermore, the nascent political concerns of *Laughable Loves* find fruition in *The Book*, Kundera's first work as an exile. The former work, to be sure, has a political element, for as Jeffery Goldfarb notes [in *Beyond Glasnost*, 1989], "The stories in *Laughable Loves* are [Kundera's] most explicitly non-political," and yet "they are about the ironies of domination and subjugation." In all these instances, however, the critique is a veiled one. *The Book*, on the other hand, attempts a much broader critique: problems of cultural heritage and national identity are explored in conjunction with a dominant event (the 1968 invasion) and a dominant theme ("organized forgetting").

Finally, the apparent aesthetic design of *The Book* makes it an example of what Ingram calls a composed cycle, while *Laughable Loves* is a completed cycle, one of "looser" design. This generic distinction is mirrored in the different quality of aesthetic experience which these works elicit in the reader—what Iser calls the "generic control of aesthetic response."

Furthermore, in his essay on Kundera, Lodge claims that "whereas in *The Joke* Kundera displayed, at the first attempt, his mastery of the modernist novel, *The Book of Laughter and Forgetting* is a masterpiece of post modem fiction ..." Similarly, I would suggest that *Laughable Loves* may be viewed as a modernist cycle, while *The Book* may be viewed as a post-modernist one.

In his later work, *The Unbearable Lightness of Being*, Kundera combines his novelistic tendencies (*The Joke, Life is Elsewhere, The Farewell Party*) with his cyclic ones, thus affecting a fusion of his various experiments with narrative architectonics. Kundera accomplishes this by returning to the essay-mode used to such great advantage in *The Book* and interweaving the essayistic sections (which are thematically anchored in the Nietzschian concept of the eternal return) with fictive events (rooted, as in *The Book*, in the 1968 invasion) concerning four central characters who serve as alternating focal points for the novel's seven parts.

As successful as Kundera's more novelistic works are, I would suggest that his two works in cyclic form are even more so, largely because of their cyclicity. Because of its paratactic superstructure, cyclic form seems to have certain advantages in describing social situations that are characterized by fragmentation and anomie and/or a narrative consciousness characterized by these qualities. As Mann notes, cycles are "especially well suited to handle certain subjects, including the sense of fragmentation or indeterminacy that many twentieth-century characters experience." And as Stevick suggests in his comments on Hemingway's cycle *In Our Time*, cyclic form may be a cognate of a given ideological construct:

> Explicitly developed progressions between narrative units imply a great deal, one hardly realizes how much until one notices their absence: they imply a coherence within the fictive world that is physical, epistemological, and moral. Most of these coherences Hemingway did not believe in and would not counterfeit. The interchapters of *In Our Time* in their relation to the stories that occur between them, are examples of a lack of faith in coherence made into a structural principle. [*The Chapter in Fiction: Theories of Narrative Division*, 1970]

Certainly, the cycle has an advantage over the novel in this regard in that it shows a broad cross-section of characters who, as in *Laughable Loves*, are isolated from one another, quite different from one another, and yet have similar, socially-determined problems.

Perhaps the two most notable story cycles are Joyce's *Dubliners* and Sherwood Anderson's *Winesburg, Ohio*. One must first note the uncanny similarity between the work of Joyce and Anderson—a coincidence that in the first decade of the twentieth century Joyce wrote a sequence of interrelated stories "depicting the drab, isolated, and frustrated citizens of Dublin and that in the next decade Anderson wrote stories of the same kind of people in a small Midwestern town" ["Sherwood Anderson and James Joyce," *American Literature* 52 (1980)]. What is even more remarkable is that in spite of the affinities between these two works, Anderson, as Curry goes to great lengths to demonstrate, was unaware of *Dubliners* at the time. This strongly suggests that cyclic form is conducive to the fictive rendering of a certain type of experience—what Joyce referred to as "paralysis" and what Anderson called the "starved side of American small town life." The formal similarity of the two works is furthermore interesting when one considers the differences between Joyce and Anderson. Joyce, on the one hand, was well-versed in aesthetic theory and often drew on this theoretical knowledge in his practice as a writer. Anderson, on the other hand, though well-read and not at all the naif he has often been regarded as, was "almost completely ignorant of aesthetic theory" (Curry). It seems, then, that even though Joyce took the "high road" of academic knowledge and Anderson took the "low road" of a strong aesthetic intuition, they both had a similar point-of-departure (anomized characters as subject) and the same point-of-arrival (cyclic form).

Another analogous work in this regard is Richard Wright's *Uncle Tom's Children*, which has been called "Wright's Dubliners" [Craig Hansen Werner, *Paradoxical Resolutions*, 1982]. In this work, Wright presents a varied cross-section of Black Americans in their struggle against oppression. The discrimination and violence faced by Black Americans is such that when one compares it to the struggles of other nationalities, one does so at the risk of trivialization. Nonetheless, it is a struggle that is not without its similarities to the Irish situation portrayed by Joyce or the Czech situation portrayed by Kundera. Wright's cycle is characterized, as is *Dubliners*, by a linear pattern of development in which each protagonist is older than his predecessor in the cycle. The first stories in this work take particular advantage of the fragmentation effect of cyclic form by showing the futility of isolated struggle while the closing stories, paralleling the reader's sense of totality, suggest the possibilities of social consciousness and collective action. As in other cycles, Wright's is characterized by what Ingram calls a "pattern of development" and what I have elsewhere called a mega-narrative: we see a trajectory which parallels the African-American's quest for freedom. As McCall points out, in each of the four stories Wright "broadens the areas of responsibility on the part of each succeeding main character, moving from boy to community leader, from victim to victor, so that the stories will compose a rising tide of militancy" [*The Example of Richard Wright*, 1969]. And again, such a social portrait seems to find its best expression in cyclic form.

Both *Laughable Loves* and *The Book* have much in common with these works by Joyce, Anderson, and Wright. For example, R. B. Gill notes a number of affinities between *The Book* and *Dubliners*. In addition to their shared formal characteristics, "both books are the work of an exile trying to make sense of his lost country and of his reasons for leaving it. Both are realistic appraisals of the paralysis that has afflicted their homelands." Furthermore, all four of these writers have endeavored to provide, among other things, a portrait of an oppressive society. They were all, in one way or another, exiles—Anderson, in a figurative sense, an exile from the trappings of small-town America; Joyce, an exile by choice from his stultifying and provincial homeland; Wright, also an exile by volition, living out the last decade of his life in France in a gesture that he had given up on the possibility of change in America; and Kundera, who, as it were, purchased his exile (also to France) through the very act of writing. After the 1970 publication of *Laughable Loves*, the Czech regime banned Kundera's works, and *The Book of Laughter and Forgetting*, published in 1979 while Kundera was living in France, caused the regime to exile him in absentia. All of these writers created works that portray what might be termed "anomized" or "paralyzed" societies as viewed by the self-exiled artist; and all these works are cycles.

To say that cyclic form is suited to a particular cultural experience and intent on the part of the author may seem to be overstating the case; after all, there are any number of novels which depict such societies, and thus it would be premature to postulate something akin to a scientific law of literary form regarding story cycles (or for that matter, any other literary phenomenon). On the other hand, I think that the affinities outlined above strike one as being something more than coincidence. Specific literary form, specific generic types, the above evidence suggests, have sociological cognates.

Which brings us to the question of genre itself. One problem with arguing that *The Book* is an example of the cycle genre is that Kundera himself prefers to call it a novel. In his view, the novel as genre is not identified by narrative continuity or for that matter any other structural feature. As he puts it, it is a mistake "to regard a certain stereo-typed structure as the inviolable essence of the novel" (*Art of the Novel*). Rather, he defines it in terms of its spirit of inquiry (which he finds particularly evident in Diderot and Sterne) and its ability both to absorb and to undermine other, dogmatic discourses.

So which is it—novel or cycle?

A generic designation is not important in and of itself. As Todorov notes, "categories have merely a constructed existence," and as a result, a work can manifest "more than one category, more than one genre" [*The Fantastic*, translated by Richard Howard, 1973]. The importance of generic designation is its heuristic value in relation to one's purpose. Mine has been to reveal the formal complexity of *Laughable Loves*, its role in Kundera's aesthetic development, the nature of the reading experience it elicits, and its similarities, in purpose and form, to a number of other notable works.

JOHN O'BRIEN

Milan Kundera: Meaning, Play, and the Role of the Author

In the world of books, the author is dead and has been for quite a while—as has the traditionally axiomatic idea that the author has some say in what is being said. Yet outside the discussions of authorship taking place within the academic circle, Milan Kundera has experienced first-hand some very real implications of being an author and writing a "dangerous" text. Because of the works he authored before the Russian invasion, Kundera was fired from his teaching post, his books were removed from libraries and universally banned, and he was denied the means to support himself. Until recently, his novels have been read in dozens of languages with the ironic exception of the language in which the novels were written.

The challenge to the common effacement of the author is more appropriately found, however, in Kundera's texts themselves. Kundera's novels give voice to a powerful intrusive author identifying himself bluntly as none other than Milan Kundera. Enriched by the more radical narrative examples of Sterne and Diderot, Kundera weaves an author-figure into his texts with stark autobiographical intrusions that threaten the provocative flippancy with which Roland Barthes announced/pronounced the demise of the author in his famous essay.

Still, on closer analysis, what Barthes says and Kundera does are not as diametrically opposed as one might assume. The focus of this analysis of

From *Critique*, Vol. XXXIV, No. 1, Fall, 1992. © 1992.

Kundera and his authorship will be to examine these issues, appropriately concentrating on the degree to which Barthes (the author's executioner) provides a valuable theoretical tool for the exploration of Kundera's authorial stance and for the kind of play that characterizes his novels. Barthes's general sense of authorship and the erotic potential of texts are strikingly close to the kind of reading Kundera's texts invite. Contrary to the position of Nina Pelikan Straus—against which much of what follows can be read—I contend that the intrusive author-figure does not work to demand a strict adherence to historical or political context. In fact, I argue that the opposite is true.

In an insightful discussion of *The Book of Laughter and Forgetting*, Nina Pelikan Straus furthers her claim that the novel is intended to be bound inextricably to Czechoslovak history, depending on the understanding that the intrusive author-figure is autobiographical in nature, not a dispersed extension or modality of the writing subject. [Straus, "Erasing History and Deconstructing the Text: Milan Kundera's *The Book of Laughter and Forgetting*," in *Critique*, Vol. 28, No. 2, pp. 69-85]. She argues that the novel consistently parodies the over-theorization of criticism to the degree that all context is lost in the rush to reveal the chaotic indeterminacy of the text. Most polemical in her attack of deconstruction, she goes so far as to claim that in the novel Kundera is speaking out directly against even the belief that no single interpretation is "right" or should be preferred over another. Straus sees deconstruction as an attempt to turn the more "obvious intentions" of *The Book* upside down, and she argues that the novel's structure and technique (including the intrusive author) are directly related to the content—the recurring, simple motif that history tends to get lost or erased by others. When she contends that the strong authorial voice functions as protection against "inhuman theories" that would insist on plural meanings, she bluntly denies Barthes in the process:

> This is not to say that the anti-deconstructionist critic has no "fun," but that his [or her] fun must be qualified by the awareness that history, and the language which ties us to history, can never quite be "jouissant"—a mere game and plaything for the mind— in the sense that Roland Barthes describes it. The dehumanization of the text into a game without reference to the facts of history is, for Kundera, simply painful.

In claiming that Kundera intends to defend against—and even to satirize—such a critical practice, Straus later argues that his texts support this agenda with his use of "authorial commentary and self-exposure":

> Inscribing himself as witness and critic of his own book, Kundera cannot but remind the reader ... [that] no reading, except what the author intends, is quite legitimate in his terms; and the facts pertinent to that reading must forever be given priority.

The voice of the intrusive author, according to Straus, is an intentional narrative device employed to make the text in-deconstructible, closed to interpretations that stray from the author's intended agenda.

My analysis is largely propelled by an interest in the question of whether Kundera's use of the intrusive author in his novels challenges the critical assumptions of "The Death of the Author" and related essays. Barthes's most direct statements on authorship correspond in broad terms to the three areas relevant in this analysis: (1) the distinction between the author (the scriptor, the writing subject) and the institutional handling of the term, (2) the author as means of foreclosing on the possibility of play, and (3) the erotic potential of writing. Looking beyond the obvious provocation, one finds in Barthes's work not so much the corpse of the writer, as the "body" reassembled/disassembled in the text itself, though with no algebraic symmetry or recognizable coherence. This "author" is not to be confused with the institutional use of the term, such as Foucault's Author-Function or any "biographical hero" (see also *The Pleasure of the Text*). The author, as Barthes uses the term, is the subject as "dispersed" in the Text, which is itself the "destroyer of all subject." The "presence" of the "author" is tolerated only insomuch as it promotes play.

The questions suggested, if Barthes is to offer a productive means of approaching Kundera's novels, are twofold: Does Kundera actually appear in the guise of direct autobiography? If he does, does the appearance act to solidify some larger meaning antithetical to Barthes's pluralism? Kundera manages to introduce to the text an author-figure far less "dispersed" than the one suggested by Barthes, while at the same time he uses the opportunity to facilitate (if not demand) play. In this way, Kundera forces a reconsideration of Barthes's theoretical stance or at least calls into question the mutual exclusivity of the bliss of indeterminacy and the existence of a strong authorial voice.

However, in direct opposition to Straus's idea that Kundera uses the author-figure to make his novels resistant to anything but interpretation firmly located in history, it is much more arguable that these intrusions add a sense of play by admitting that characters are not real, questioning motivations, digressing, telling stories, and so on. Although some stories are historically placed, that fact does not mean that they or the author-figure are immovable or in any way privileged. The clearest aim is not to provide answers but to question, and this view is most consistently reflected in the novels' treatment of characterization and theme. Where Straus concludes it must be "painful" for Milan Kundera to see his work taken out of what she sees as its proper context, the interview reprinted immediately after the text of *The Book of Laughter and Forgetting* (the "Afterword") addresses this kind of reading, locating whatever pain he might experience elsewhere: "The stupidity of the world comes from having an answer for everything. The wisdom of the novel comes from having a question for everything."

In this light, Milan Kundera must be seen as an advocate, not for historical context, but for the kind of interrogation underscored repeatedly by his novels and his polemical statements made in interviews. In particular, the intrusive and inimitable voice of Kundera as author stirs up the text. Take out this intrusive dynamic, and the text is far less radical because it is precisely this "I" that rips away the facade of verisimilitude, that questions the possibility of meaning, and that carries through a recognizable disgust for any system that refuses free play with codes—whether political (Communist or Western), linguistic, or literary. Literature that only provides answers would be as totalitarian as the regime Kundera left behind, and Barthes, too, stresses this capability of writing:

> Writing is the art of asking questions, not of answering or resolving them. Only writing can ask a question, and because writing has this power, it can afford to leave questions in abeyance.... When a work is successful, it asks its question with ambiguity and, in that way, becomes poetic. (*The Grain*)

It may be that the political events around and after 1968 provide a convenient and concrete historical framework that is meaningful, but to translate Kundera's use of historical reference points as a maneuver of closure is simply a more refined way of saying that a text can be read in one way only.

To some extent, the question of the necessity of looking outside the text for historical context is a moot point. The texts provide such reference points internally. Kundera discusses the problem and his use of history in his preface to *Life Is Elsewhere*:

> Even though the story of Jaromil and his mother takes place in a specific historic period which is portrayed truthfully (without the slightest satiric intent), it was not my aim to describe a period....

In other words: for a novelist, a given historic situation is an anthropologic laboratory in which he explores his basic question: What is human existence? In the case of this novel, several related questions also presented themselves.... The novel, of course, does not answer any of these questions.

So, one must question the appropriateness of Straus's characterization of Kundera's pain or her own general sense of urgency, her fear that somehow history is going to be airbrushed out of existence as in the falsified photos mentioned in the vignette opening *The Book of Laughter and Forgetting*.

Actually, there is reason to believe that, of all the interesting and viable implications of the intrusive author, an emphasis on historical context— which must occur at the expense of play—is neither a sufficient explanation of the author-figure's function in the text nor (for what it's worth) close to the agenda of the Kundera who wrote the novels. Such historical placement of the characters amounts to little more than the equivalent of a minimal backdrop or collection of props to stage a drama, and Kundera concludes that the novel that merely illustrates a historical situation is severely limited. Contrary to Straus's contention that the "text is nothing but an effort to recoup literature from its modern self-enclosure and to tie it as closely as possible to physically experienced history," historical context is "secondary matter" to what Kundera calls the problems of existence that he repeatedly stresses are his only interest.

As one might expect of any writer, Kundera repeatedly resists pigeonholing or what he calls "the termites of reduction," and, in comment after comment, he posits the writer as far outside the field of commitment as Barthes did the writers of the New Novel. Perhaps Kundera is even more provocative:

> If you cannot view the art that comes to you from Prague, Budapest, or Warsaw in any other way than by means of this wretched political code, you murder it, no less brutally than the worst of the Stalinist dogmatists. And you are quite unable to hear its true voice. The importance of this art does not lie in the fact that it pillories this or that political regime but that, on the strength of social and human experience of a kind people here in the West cannot even imagine, it offers a new testimony about mankind.

In numerous theoretical discussions, Kundera speaks of the need to revitalize the novel in what amounts to the direction of noncommitment, arguing that the "voice of the novel" is hard to hear over the temptation to find any or especially a single truth. The result is a plea to indeterminacy:

> A novel does not assert anything; a novel searches and poses questions. I don't know whether my nation will perish and I don't know which of my characters is right. I invent stories, confront one with another, and by this means I ask questions ... The novelist teaches the reader to comprehend the world as a question ... In a world built on sacrosanct certainties the novel is dead. The totalitarian world, whether founded on Marx, Islam, or anything else, is a world of answers rather than questions. There, the novel has no place.

History is important, but only inasmuch as it facilitates insights into self-consciously imagined characters.

Therefore, Kundera's vision of the literary possibilities coincides with Barthes's understanding that the text should enjoy a displacement from social responsibility, play instead of commitment, and eventually (ideally) the bliss of complete hedonistic detachment. Kundera's works share the emphasis of text over context and do so unapologetically at the expense of meaning. Kimball's basic observations in his analysis of ambiguity in Kundera's writing are accurate ["The Ambiguities of Milan Kundera," *New Criterion*, Vol. 4, No. 5, January, 1986, pp. 5-13]. Though he later accuses the author of "transcendental buffoonery" in his aloofness regarding his writing from any "definite commitment," he correctly highlights the problematic nature of the "terminal paradox" that Kundera embraces: "[Kundera wants] to have it both ways: he wants both the freedom of fiction and the authority of historical fact." Yet the problem begs the question that is fairly resolved when one is reminded that when Kundera talks about the novel in general and his novels in particular, he speaks similarly of his writing not as a "rebus to be decoded" but as a game, sounding all the while unmistakably like one of Barthes's reveries on the pleasure of the text when he says a novel is "a game with invented characters ... [that gives you] the joy of imagination, of narration, the joy provided by a game. That is how I see a novel—as a game."

Kundera's penchant for asking questions instead of answering them, combined with an episodic structure and lack of temporal coherence, assures ellipses and ambiguity; this much is self-evident. The effect of the intrusive author-figure, however, is more complicated. Does this author/ narrator, as one would expect (and Straus demands), work to pull the disparate fragments together? However philosophically difficult the notion of one demonstrable self may be, it must be admitted that the authorial voice is a relatively stable feature of a narrative strategy that constantly changes almost everything else. Yet when that voice digresses or asks broad metaphysical questions, the voice of the author-figure works to prevent prefigured answers to a text of questions:

> Why is Tamina on a children's island? Why is that where I imagine her?

> I don't know.

Kundera exploits this technique repeatedly to assert his aesthetics of ambiguity. The same chapter/fragment that tells of the death of Tereza's dog is interwoven with essayistic authorial commentary, including a story of Nietzsche's stopping the beating of a horse with a tearful embrace. To some extent, the authorial digressions and intrusions add to a certain thematic unity, but only in that they sometimes share a tangential connection; they do not contribute to an understanding as much as they are inconclusive in comparably similar ways. Lodge agrees in "Milan Kundera and the Idea of the Author in Modern Criticism," when he mentions that "paradoxically, this overt appearance of the author in the text does not make it easier, but harder, to determine what it 'means'" [*Critical Quarterly*, Vol. 26, Nos. 1-2, 1984, pp. 105-21].

Finally, there is in Kundera's work also a decidedly self-conscious effort toward elaborate linguistic play, an acknowledgment on the level of content and presentation that language is itself indeterminate. Room for plural interpretation and erotic bliss is cleared away in the unpredictable space between the shifting allegiances of signifier and signified. Just as the questions that the novels pose offer myriad possible answers (or none), there is a kind of unsettling recognition in the language of the texts and their parenthetical clarifications of the arbitrary nature of language. The most obvious display of this modern/postmodern notion is in *The Unbearable Lightness of Being*, especially in the linguistic problems in the relationship of Franz and Sabina.

The unforgettable feature of the time Sabina and Franz share together is the frequency of their inability to understand each other, and that misunderstanding has everything to do with semiotics: "If [people] meet when they are older, like Franz and Sabina, the [musical compositions of their lives] are more or less complete, and every motif, every object, every word means something different to each of them." And elsewhere: "Although they had a clear understanding of the logical meaning of the words they exchanged, they failed to hear the semantic susurrus of the river flowing through them." Kundera generates an ironically lengthy *Short Dictionary of Misunderstood Words* to take up systematically the topic of their drastically mismatched systems of codes. Indeed, the novel goes further to include discussion of images as signs, pointing out that the meaning of a particular sign—the bowler hat in particular—not only means different things to different people, but also different things at different times to the same person:

Each time the same object would give rise to a new meaning, though all former meanings would resonate (like an echo, like a parade of echoes) together with a new one. Each new experience would resound, each time enriching the harmony.

The same phenomenon is found in *The Book of Laughter and Forgetting*, for example, in the parodic section "The Angels," where two American students are giving an oral report for their favorite teacher on Ionesco's *Rhinoceros*. In their conversation, the two girls stumble on the arbitrary nature of semiotics:

"I'm not so sure I understand what all those people turning into rhinoceroses is supposed to mean," said Gabrielle.
"Think of it as a symbol," Michelle told her.
"True," said Gabrielle, "literature is a system of signs."
"And the rhinoceros is first and foremost a sign," said Michelle.
"Yes, but even if we accept the fact they turn into signs instead of rhinoceroses, how do they choose what signs to turn into?"
"Yes, well, that's a problem," said Michelle sadly. They were on their way back to the dormitory and walked awhile in silence.

It is a problem that is never clarified, and the story of two girls trying to figure out what it all means finally, after repeated interruption, reaches a dramatic conclusion, but even that is inconclusive. The girls give their report wearing cardboard rhino horns, but, the author-figure volunteers, it is as embarrassing as if a man had stood up in front of the class and shown off his amputated arm. Still, the girls accept the laughter of their teacher as a sign of encouragement. Next, a girl in the class who hates the two Americans calmly walks to the front of the class and kicks them one at a time, then returns to her seat. The girls read her sign clearly enough (you are making fools of yourself, and I hate you), but the teacher, assuming the kick is a planned part of the presentation, laughs all the more. A surrealist finale of semiotic confusion builds and concludes the story. The kick is the crux of the scene. It promptly recalls the girls' realization that language is no longer working (the class missed their point that the play was comic and instead thought the girls were embarrassingly ludicrous). Without the kick, the miscommunication is ironic, but with it the irony is amplified to a tragic comedy on the failure of language.

Always there is an inherent contradiction in these kinds of critical analyses that take pages upon pages to argue that a novel does not mean anything. So, if only to validate the critical act that Straus so powerfully denies, it is tempting to qualify somewhat—even though Barthes would see no need to justify the text that creates bliss. If Kundera calls into question the ability of his texts to reflect any single truth, interpretation, or historical/political context, many less-Epicurean readers will start to wonder: (1) If the novelist is not only "nobody's spokesman," but—according to Kundera—"not even the spokesman for his own ideas," why should we bother to read the author's books? (2) Is such a maneuver an attempt to shrug off responsibility for what the novel might seem to mean or promote, such as the over-worn and even offensive sexual stereotypes that Kundera's novels seem to perpetuate?

The texts, though fragmented and drastically nonlinear, are hardly complete anarchy. So when the author-figure speaks in *The Book of Laughter and Forgetting* of an equilibrium of power between "too much uncontested meaning on earth" and the world if it "loses all its meaning," an accurate schematic of the tensions of Kundera's writing might be drawn. An analysis of the sexual politics of his work can function both as an attempt to justify reading novels that question the ability to communicate in a systematically productive way and as an attempt to suggest that his merciless contesting of meaning works to overturn other points where the texts may offer more-or-less misogynist representations.

Initially, however, one way to understand more exactly the way in which Barthes's aesthetics of bliss lives within this apparent contradiction is to look at the traditional approach to literary aesthetics, such as that described in Ames's *Aesthetics of the Novel* (1928), where a distinction is drawn between the sensuality of the plastic arts and the primarily social value of literature: "If the test of sensuous art is in its effect upon the physical self, the test of literature must be in its effect upon the social self." Consequently a "beautiful book" is one that evokes a deep social response, which "ministers better to the modern self than any art"; such a book suggests "harmonies unheard." Ames suggests that modern art employs sensuality in language, but in the Machiavellian style of Shaw or Brecht, in order to lure the reader/audience into becoming receptive to the social message. Consequently, "the weakness of much modern art lies in its lack of purpose beyond giving a sensuous impression, which by itself cannot possibly absorb a social being."

Barthes and Kundera present an opposite aesthetic understanding that savors the fact that a text is beyond any such social responsibility. Bliss thrives on contradiction, including the admitted cohabitation within the text of both the revolutionary and the asocial. In fact, for Barthes, this edge defines the "site of bliss" itself. When Kimball claims that Kundera "wants it both ways," he focuses on the novels' ambiguity, identifying an erotic surface blasphemously inscribed with distractions and abrasions—what Barthes calls the seam where meaning is lost and everything clashes. This fault line in Kundera's novels is underscored by the intrusive author, who repeatedly strips away false simplicity to reveal not a smooth, codified continuity but a clash of codes and cliché much in the spirit of Sabina's maxim: "On the surface, an intelligible lie; underneath, the unintelligible truth."

Literal eroticism (here in the physical sense) is central to Kundera's novels. In part, the unrestrained sexual honesty is responsible for his success, but it also creates problems when the texts seem guilty of propagating sexist stereotypes as readers' sensitivity to matters of gender continues to improve. However, a reading of the novels, combined with an understanding of the kind of play elaborated upon here, suggests that the handling of gender roles and sexual stereotypes in the novels can arguably work to up-end sexist foundations—a specific example of play at work, inverting instead of affirming codes and stereotypes. Just as his novels resist the dissident stereotype in their refusal to accept the good guy/bad guy (Western/Communist) hierarchy that many readers never move beyond, the seeming weak woman/strong man (Tereza/Tomas, Marketa/Karel) misogynist surface of the texts is more likely just that, a surface smooth only from a distance.

With its moment of dislocation and hedonistic incoherence, the sexual act is, in Kundera's novels, a crucial point for precisely the reasons Barthes draws on this metaphor for his articulation of bliss. In an ironic gesture of conjugation, all semiotic systems fall apart in dislocating sexual bliss, leaving contradictions both revealed and reveled in. Appropriately, Kundera describes his erotic scenes as generating an "extremely sharp light which suddenly reveals the essence of characters" and goes on to cite the example of Tamina's making love to Hugo while she thinks about "lost vacations with her dead husband." He repeats the theme in *The Unbearable Lightness of Being* when Tereza makes loveless love to the engineer; here, too, there is no joining or communication beyond the physical coupling, and this event is simply a representation of what happens throughout the novels on levels more subtle than this obvious example of two people making love for not only different but contradictory reasons. Kundera, therefore, resists the use of stereotypes, as discussed by Barthes in *The Pleasure of the Text*, where he recognizes "the bliss repressed beneath the stereotype."

It stands to reason that if, as earlier discussed in relation to the *Short Dictionary of Misunderstood Words*, language fails, the cultural and sexual codes and stereotypes constructed from/in language must fail, too. A naive reading of a Kundera text "as though it were natural" (Barthes's definition of the stereotype) abounds with the type of sexual cliché exemplified by Kael's review of the film:

> But the young Binoche [Tereza] gives the role a sweet gaucheness and then a red-cheeked desperation.... She verges on peasant-madonna darlingness, but that's what the conception requires [*New Yorker*, February 8, 1988, pp. 67-70].

Allowing the termites of reduction to go to work will produce a weak character in Tereza and a Don Juan in Tomas, but clearly beneath the surface of such a reading lies the kind of complex contradiction and "terminal paradox" that Edmund White enjoys when he writes that "Kundera's heroes may be Don Juans, but they are shy, apologetic ones; his women are intensely physical beings, but they are also as quirkily intelligent and stubbornly independent as his men." Following the social script, Tereza also sees herself as weak and Tomas strong, but her epiphany, pages before the end of the novel, betrays the inadequacy of the signifiers "weak" and "strong" to explain the complexity of the apparently simple roles. And it is the intrusive author again who brings the reader to examine the issue directly:

> We all have a tendency to consider strength the culprit and weakness the innocent victim. But now Tereza realized that in her case the opposite was true! Even her dreams, as if aware of the single weakness in a man otherwise strong, made a display of her suffering to him, thereby forcing him to retreat. Her weakness was aggressive and kept forcing him to capitulate until eventually he lost his strength and was transformed into the rabbit in her arms.

Furthermore, weakness in the texts is hardly gender specific. It is, after all, Sabina who is the epitome of "lightness," with her chronology of betrayals. In Franz is found the inversion of the stereotype suggested by Tereza. Defining love as the expectation of rejection and the renunciation of strength, Franz ultimately is abandoned by both mistress (Sabina) and wife:

[For Franz, love] meant a longing to put himself at the mercy of his partner. He who gives himself up like a prisoner of war must give up his weapons as well. And deprived in advance of defense against a possible blow, he cannot help wondering when the blow will fall. That is why I can say that for Franz, love meant the constant expectation of a blow.

Straus claims that Kundera wishes to "insure that his own discourse will not be deconstructed or its meaning erased." Although the assertion may be primarily motivated by a desire to refute deconstruction (for whatever reason), the intrusive author presents codes and roles in what amount to an already-deconstructed form.

This play, especially in matters as grave as gender-based oppression and exploitation, is necessarily not always playful in a humorous sense. However, that which results from the breakdown of semiotic systems is central to the comic/ironic perspective of all Kundera's works as far back as his first collection of short stories tellingly titled *Laughable Loves*, where a cynical comic vision hinges on the stereotype or the cliché. As Barthes is interested in innocent language being twisted out of proportion and into bliss, Kundera's comedy resides in the condition of characters who live codes and gender roles as if they were Truth ("as if they were natural"). His short story "The Hitchhiking Game" is an ideal example in the way it begins with a much-abused erotic cliché (picking up the pretty hitchhiker) but ends with a tragic misunderstanding. They are actually lovers on vacation playing a role-change game during a long drive, the girl pretending to be a promiscuous hitchhiker when she is really "old-fashioned." The power of codes is, in these texts, most forcefully revealed when the codes are split open by a realization as dramatic as the already-mentioned kick.

It is fair to say that in writing that is interested in depicting sexuality in an honest way, clichés, restrictive gender roles, and stereotypes that set one's teeth on edge will most likely be included among the props. But if Kundera doesn't slip from them by openly divulging their contradictions, it might be in part a result of the infestation of archaic codes in language, for they are shown consistently to be inverted and subverted just below the surface of the texts themselves.

One final point at which the erotic textual qualities come in contact with the actual erotic themes of the novels is in the repeated associations with the terms "weight" and "lightness." It is possible to interpret these two opposites (among, of course, the infinite possibilities) as alluding to the "weight" of uncontested meaning and eternal return and the "lightness" of a world or a text without meaning. Thus, it is possible to equate Tomas's infidelity and numerous erotic friendships as a rejection of the temptation to believe in a single interpretation of truth. Furthermore, the vacillation of Tomas between lightness and weight could simply represent an extension of humanity's attempt to reach an equilibrium between these diametrically opposed but equally unbearable epistemological attitudes. In contrast to the lightness of the signifier's "instant, not consistent, relationships," Barthes, too, associates weight with stabilized meaning. When Kimball, then, notices that if Kundera's work is a game it is deprived of "authority and weight," it is easy to see that this fact, along with his choice of metaphors, may be exactly what Kundera (not to mention Barthes) would be happy to hear.

Surely it should not be assumed that to grant the obvious, that the author-figure in these texts is a more dynamic, self-acknowledged "author," is somehow to elevate the author to status beyond that of what Barthes calls the "paper character," especially when that figure repeatedly reasserts a textual playground on various levels (linguistic play and play with the semiotic structures that form the foundations of culture). What Kundera calls the joy of a game and Barthes calls bliss is that which flies in the face of meaning and the expectation of meaning—that which condemns mere consumption and promotes nothing but its own indeterminacy.

In a way, the figure of the author substitutes for traditional historical context, but this author-figure in the texts does not "bring things together." He is not functioning in a way as to reinstitute "man-and-his-work criticism" or to resurrect Herder's view of reading as "divination into the soul of the creator." True, much apparently autobiographical matter is presented, but these events are treated, as are the historical ones, as points for questions. At every turn, like the narrator in *Tristram Shandy*, the author-figure digresses, interrupts, tells stories, meditates, extrapolates, and interpolates—encouraging the same relationship with his text as that of a reader of a text of bliss: "What I enjoy in a narrative is not directly its content or even its structure, but rather the abrasions I impose upon the fine surface: I read on, I skip, I look up, I dip in again." And if the resulting questions, contradictions, and lack of clear context deprive the reader of recognizable reference points, this also serves to discourage thoughtless consumption. The resulting ambiguity and lack of commitment are not, after all, what consumers expect.

If, however, the analogy is valid and the author-figure in the text acts as a kind of preacher of indeterminacy, it should be mentioned that the texts more correctly preach against the imposition of meaning rather than the entire possibility that some stabilization of meaning might take place. They are not as much nihilist as they are deferring to the reader, paralleling the changing of the guard that concludes "The Death of the Author." It is not surprising that this kind of move would anger those with very specific interpretive agendas—like Podhoretz who scolds Kundera's for his political aloofness, which he maintains is nothing short of "cooperating with your own kidnappers." In fact, by winding the reader through a vertiginous array of perspectives and questions, the urgency to find an answer is itself lost, as is the necessity to divide existence into binary oppositions. Finally, Barthes would undoubtedly see this very representative maneuver as the kind of "violence that enables [the text] to exceed the laws that a society, an ideology, a philosophy establish for themselves in order to agree among themselves in a fine surge of historical intelligibility. This excess is called: writing."

POSTSCRIPT: KUNDERA'S IMMORTALITY

This analysis of play, intrusive authorship, and the significance of history in Kundera's fiction has focused considerably on *The Book of Laughter and Forgetting* and *The Unbearable Lightness of Being*, but Kundera's novels develop contrapuntal patterns and motifs both within and between his particular texts. For example, one could hardly manage a comprehensive analysis of history without discussing *The Joke* at length, where, "the joke" is History. Similarly, questions about Kundera's intrusive stance in his fiction would need to look to his latest effort, *Immortality*. Here, the intrusive author is not only named "Milan Kundera" but compares characters in this book to characters in earlier books and lends a copy of *Life Is Elsewhere* to another character (who never reads it). *Immortality* is also Kundera's most extended attempt to discuss directly the significance of the author in interpretation. In particular, the novel strongly argues against the idea that interpretation should be constrained by historical or biographical contexts.

Hemingway laments to Goethe how "instead of reading my books, they're writing books about me," with specific disgust aimed at the "army of university professors all over America ... busy classifying, analyzing, and shoveling everything into articles and books." And Goethe answers by retelling his nightmare of theater fans that come to see a puppet show of his Faust:

> I turned around and I was aghast: I expected them out front,
> and instead they were at the back of the stage, gazing at me with

wide-open, inquisitive eyes. As soon as my glance met theirs, they began to applaud. And I realized that my Faust didn't interest them all and that the show they wished to see was not the puppets I was leading around the stage, but me myself! Not Faust, but Goethe.... I realized that I would never get rid of them, never, never, never.

As if finally to underscore his assertion that actual authors who produce texts should not be confused with whatever/whoever appears in those texts, Goethe aggressively argues the point even further than Hemingway:

> "Forget for a moment that you're an American and exercise your brain: he who doesn't exist cannot be present. Is that so complicated? The instant I died I vanished from everywhere, totally. I even vanished from my books. Those books exist in the world without me. Nobody will ever find me in them.... Don't make a fool of yourself, Ernest," said Goethe. "You know perfectly well that at this moment we are but the frivolous fantasy of a novelist who lets us say things we would probably never say on our own."

If the surreal conversation of two dead, distant authors is not concrete enough to make clear what is "painful" in the eyes of "Milan Kundera," Paul's long, drunken speech near the end of the novel is an exaggerated characterization of biographical reading:

> We started to talk about all sorts of things. Avenarius referred a few more times to my novels, which he had not read, and so provoked Paul to make a remark whose rudeness astonished me: "I don't read novels. Memoirs are much more amusing and instructive for me. Or biographies. Recently I've been reading books about Salinger, Rodin, and the loves of Franz Kafka. And a marvelous biography of Hemingway. What a fraud. What a liar. What a megalomaniac." Paul laughed happily. "What an impotent. What a sadist. What a macho. What an erotomaniac. What a misogynist."

Immortality, then, argues forcefully both against privileging contextual interpretation and for a playful irresponsibility in the relationship between the author and the authored text. It is not historical context itself that runs contrary to the kind of interpretation I think Kundera's texts invite, but interpretation that exclusively privileges the prop or backdrop at the expense of the questions that resonate beyond both history and authorship.

TOM WILHELMUS

Time and Distance

In *Thus Spoke Zarathustra*, the animals say to Nietzsche's philosopher-mystic:

> "Look, we know what you teach: that all things return forever,
> and we along with them, and that we have already been here an
> infinite number of times, and all things along with us."

According to Milan Kundera, this "mad myth" is Nietzsche's means of forcing us to contemplate the horror as well as the beauty and sublimity of life's events in a way which prevents our overlooking them because they are so fleeting. Without some such concept—that an event may return again and again to haunt us—"We would need take no more note of it than of a war between two African kingdoms in the fourteenth century, a war that altered nothing in the destiny of the world, even if a hundred thousand blacks perished in excruciating torment" (*The Unbearable Lightness of Being*). Repetition, recurrence, the myth of eternal return show the weight of history and create the awareness that life has significance and depth. In some fashion, this fact is illustrated in each of the works which follow. Each is concerned with time, and each creates perspective and distance. Each also deals with recurrence, without which time itself is only duration.

From *The Hudson Review*, Vol. XLVI, No. 1, Spring, 1993. © 1978 by *The Hudson Review*.

[When] it originally came out—in Czechoslovakia in 1965—the publication of Kundera's *The Joke*, must have seemed like a miracle, though with the crackdown following the Prague Spring three years later, it was one of the first works suppressed and its author banned. In the space remaining, I cannot treat the details that have made the new "definitive" version of *The Joke* necessary. But since the recent events in Eastern Europe and the Soviet Union, it may be time to re-read the novel anyway, for in the interim, history has played an even greater joke on Communism itself, and Kundera's reflections may provide a hint as to why it occurred.

The novel begins as its principal character Ludvik stands at a crossroads in a small Moravian village where he grew up on the day before a festival celebrating the traditional Ride of the Kings, a folk ritual from the remote past. Ludvik, however, has come home primarily to carry out a private act of revenge against someone who had played an important role in the most significant event of his life—his expulsion from the university and from the Party for playing a stupid, adolescent joke. The joke had consisted of sending a postcard with some anti-Party slogans on it to a girl he was courting, and Ludvik means to cuckold the party official who had an opportunity to prevent Ludvik's expulsion but who had engineered it instead. In the town he also sees people from his youth whom he had left when as a student he went to Prague.

Actually, three types of history are present in Ludvik's situation: personal, political, and Moravian. The latter includes the folk traditions inherent in the "Ride of the Kings" as well as comments about folk music and Christianity later in the novel. Each type of history represents a form of recurrence that Ludvik would rather be without. The desire to lay the blame for all his failures on a single absurd event in the past, always before his eyes, has led him to pursue a needless act of revenge. Communism, "official history," has meant that once out of the Party he has no place in history. And the nostalgic belief in "origins" seems like mindless obedience to a set of rituals repeated aimlessly from the past. During a moment of revelation late in the novel, Ludvik says:

> Yes, suddenly I saw it clearly: most people deceive themselves with a pair of faiths: they believe in eternal memory (of people, things, deeds, nations) and in redressibility (of deeds, mistakes, sins, wrongs).... [Whereas] In reality the opposite is true: everything will be forgotten and nothing will be redressed.

And, in fact, Ludvik's revenge fails, even at the moment of his success. No longer a serious threat, Communism too becomes irrelevant to his personal life. And the "Ride of the Kings" will always contain a message which "will never be decoded, not only because there is no key to it, but also because people have no patience to listen."

Yet as in most of his novels since *The Joke* this vision of the quixotic unreliability of history is as liberating as it is a source of despair. Long before the current breakup of the Eastern bloc, the Hungarian Gyorgy Konrad's classic Anti-Politics argued that Russian-style, "official" Communism would increasingly become irrelevant because people would find the means to create spontaneous unofficial social, political, and economic organizations within the official state. And just as a country cannot do without some kind of organization it cannot eliminate history either.

History, recurrence, creates weight and depth and perspective. Painful as such knowledge may be, it provides us with identity and community, two things we will always need. Nonetheless, like Ludvik, we might prefer a version of history which is more humane, essentially private, contingent, semi-official, made up on the run. Perhaps that is what Eastern Europe is learning now, though it is a view of things which, like Nietzsche's myth of eternal return, may essentially be mad.

VICKI ADAMS

Milan Kundera: The Search for Self
in a Post-Modern World

Carlos Fuentes has said that the most urgent poles of contemporary narrative are found in Latin America and in Central Europe, and the modern reader automatically thinks of Gabriel García Márquez and Milan Kundera. This paper will look at one of these well-known authors, Milan Kundera, in terms of the Slavic soul representing its geographic standing between East (the land of orthodoxy or ideology), and West (the land of nihilism). Kundera is interesting in this connection because he resists either camp: what he calls the angelic laughter of certainty, of truth, of ideology, and the demonic laughter of infinite relativism, cynicism, and nihilism we have heard so much about in Western philosophy.

Milan Kundera, the Czech writer who has been living in Paris for more than twenty years, and writing for a foreign audience because his books were banned in his own land, does lean toward the abyss (nihilism), does favor what R. B. Gill has called "epicurean accommodation," does opt for the novel of relative truths, but somehow has managed to keep a foothold on the cliff overhanging the modern abyss of nothingness. His particular foothold seems to be a rediscovery of his folk culture, as the comforts found in his early Moravian roots offer him touchstones of identity perhaps not available to other contemporary writers. His philosophical novels offer a compromise between memory and forgetting, between irony and commitment. What

From *Imagination, Emblems and Expressions: Essays on Latin American, Caribbean, and Continental Culture and Identity*, edited by Helen Ryan-Ranson, Bowling Green State University Popular Press, 1993. © 1993 by Bowling Green State University Popular Press.

might be so fetching about this writer is that, instead of arriving at the modern conclusion that life has less and less meaning in a post-Derridian world, he celebrates those very weaknesses that make us human (angst, confusion, hopelessness, uncertainty, and especially, man's simplicity) as synonymous with beauty. Thus, he turns the modern philosophical world topsy-turvy, because aesthetics has a way of turning to ethics in his post modern fiction ... his post-structuralist worldview emphasizes the beauty of the uncertainty. Unlike other modern spokesmen of a bleak and dreary reality, his acceptance of relative truths seems to be a manifestation of a wry Kunderian accommodation to man's powerlessness in post-Stalinist Central Europe.

The goal of this paper is to underscore the role of Kundera's folk heritage in the formation of his world view in his search for self and, in doing that, to consider the source of his international appeal. The investigation will first of all consider Kundera as firmly in the post-modernist camp and then look at some of Kundera's own theoretical statements on fiction and the novel (including revelatory excerpts from six of his novels). Attempting to show how his chosen form of expression—the novel—is the only one capable of expressing his concept of identity in a post-modern world, a transition will then be made from the seemingly value-free post-modern viewpoint to Kundera's other side—where his individual characters are called upon to make choices, and where the destinies of "Der Volk" matter intensely. The transition will use some very recent ideas of Derrida and Lyotard to pose the obvious question: How can a novelist, clearly so post-modern in his techniques and philosophical thrust, be at the same time a heralder of the beauty in a life chock full of irony and chaos?

Jacques Derrida offers a justification for deconstructionist thought in our world that Kundera will echo in both his novels and his own critical writings. If the truth of reason is really our own experience of it, it is relative anyway. So, we need new kinds of "knowledge" to deal with this relative world, new unheard of thoughts, "qui se cherchent agrave; travers la memoire des vieux signes" [sought from the memories of old signs]. This is precisely what Kundera will discover in his folk culture—memories of old signs—which will offer the possibility of an identity, a spiritual or psychological homeland waiting to be repossessed by him.

In terms of history (and Kundera is mainly concerned with man's relationship to the past, to history), his theory was already introduced by Foucault's deconstructionist views that it is just possible that history is made up of interpretation, not fact; that any sign/event is already an interpretation of another sign/event. The goal of history has always been the triumph of meaning, annihilation of the negative, the presence of a truth; but, when this happens, according to the deconstructionists, there is nothing left to do, nothing more to learn. Kundera's view of history has more to do with disorder than triumph of meaning. While his sentimental side yearns for a safe, unchanging, constantly returning, idyllic past, his skepticism tells us that Foucault's view was right: alternative accounts are possible when authorities in Czechoslovakia tear down the old heroic monuments, give the streets new Russian names, and fabricate in the schools a tidy and sentimental account of Czech history. Kundera writes his fiction to awaken doubts or skepticism as an alternative. He insists that the novel is the form to express this doubt, or contradiction. The novel teaches us to comprehend other peoples' truths and the limitations of our own truth, so the novel should be deeply non-ideological: "it is as essential to our insanely ideological world as is bread" ["Interview," *Le Monde*, Vol. 23, January, 1976]. In another article, "Man Thinks, God Laughs," he says that the novel's wisdom is different from that of philosophy—it is born of the spirit of humor. The novel contradicts ideological certitudes: "Like Penelope, it undoes each night the tapestry that ... philosophy and learned men wove the day before." Life is seen rationally, as a:

> glowing trajectory of causes and effects, failures, and successes, and man, setting his impatient gaze on the causal chain of his actions, accelerates further his mad race toward death.

Kundera sees human existence (its beauty) located "where the bridge between a cause and an effect is ruptured." At this juncture, there is liberty, digression, the incalculable, a lack of reason, the opposite of eighteenth-century rationalism and Liebniz. So the art born of God's laughter—the novel—is the "art that has managed to create the ... imaginative realm where no one is the possessor of the truth, and there everyone has the right to be understood." Clearly, Foucault's view of history as interpretation, or as "alternative accounts" is manifested in this 1985 essay by Kundera [*New York Review of Books*, June 13, 1985; reprinted in *The Art of the Novel*].

In Kundera's own fiction, one strongly senses a deconstructionist view of the modern world and an example of Kundera's attempt to deal with the concept of identity in this deconstructed world of his novels. In his 1973 *Life Is Elsewhere*, the theme is that the poetic viewpoint should not dominate one's life because it is incapable of irony; its only goal is beauty. Because lyricism is never ironic, it risks being totalitarian. In this novel, Jaromil, the young poet, cannot draw human faces, giving the reader a metaphor for an ideology—where only causes, and not individuals, exist, where nuance and irony are absent. At one point the narrator says of Jaromil:

> The raw simplicity of the statement made him happy because it placed him in the ranks of those direct and simple men who laughed at nuances and whose wisdom lies in their understanding of the ridiculously simple essentials of life.

Speaking later in the novel of the "adult world" of relativity, Kundera compares it with poetic form:

> In rhyme and rhythm reside a certain magical power. An amorphous world becomes at once orderly, lucid and clear, and beautiful when squeezed into regular meters. Death is chaotic, but if it is in rhyme, it is orderly.

He goes on later to say: "The adult world knows perfectly well that the absolute is an illusion, that nothing human is either great or eternal."

In *Laughable Loves* (1974) Kundera portrays love as a meaningless game, but one area of life where we are convinced we have some control, one area (along with religion) where we try to find our essence, our peculiar identity. Man has little control over most spheres of life, but in love, there is a sense of relative freedom, and that being so, women became, for one of his characters, the "one legitimate criterion of his life's destiny." Women became, for the protagonist, a way of choosing his identity in a society where he was, in every other way, powerless to express himself. Later in the same story, however, the same character complains:

All at once I understood that it had only been my illusion that we ourselves saddle events, and are able to control their course. The truth is that they aren't our stories at all, that they are foisted upon us from somewhere outside, that we are not to blame for the queer path they follow.

The interesting, diverse group of characters in *The Farewell Party* (1976) try to control their destinies in a fertility clinic where sex is used to trick destiny. They gather to say good-bye to a comrade who has gotten permission to emigrate, and the themes are similar to those in his other novels. One character says: "We really had no choices," after he had carried with him what he thought was a suicide pill for years, feeling that at least in the end, if things turned bad, he could decide his own life or death. The doctor who gave him the pill explains: "... the fake pill allowed him to turn his life into a noble myth," the myth of some control over his destiny. Kundera has also created characters in his novels who equate order with identity, who need to have the authorities establish their identities. An outspoken, and very ideological nurse at the clinic dislikes the emigré's face because it looks "ironic" to her, and she hates irony. All irony was, for her, "like an armed watchman guarding the portal to her future, disdainfully refusing her admittance." Admittance to what? To Kundera's adulthood of irony, or uncertainty, to real life? Kundera asks, "What motivates people to totalitarianism? The longing for order, the desire to turn the human world into an inorganic one?" This kind of Kunderian character needs her identity established for her; she fears that in freedom, in the chaos of uncertainty, she will not know who she is. For Kundera, real life is disorder, chaos, while a willfully imposed order is akin to death.

Kundera's two most successful novels are *The Book of Laughter and Forgetting*, published in 1978, and *The Unbearable Lightness of Being*, published in 1984. Both texts are concerned with man's relationship to history and both texts resist a single reading. Both texts need to be considered in any discussion of problems of identity because Kundera himself has equated the absurd chaos in historical events with an individual's life. The two novels keep insisting that understanding the absurdity, the lack of a rational structure in historical events is just one more way to understand his concept of individual identity. Both are inaccessible to our human understanding. The structuralists' view of history is just as mistaken as the poetic view of individual identity: rational cause and effect in history is just as illusory as is the absolute (he would say, childish) concept of apprehending one's individual identity, of knowing who we really are. Control over history and individual identity is a fiction. Both novels place their protagonists in a world where the border is warped between reality and art, or between history and the fantastic, between memory and forgetting. *The Book of Laughter and Forgetting* is called by David Lodge, "a masterpiece of post-modernist fiction." The novel offers several separate stories, some having the same characters which flow (or, as Lodge puts it, "leak") into each other. Themes, motifs and author's comments are repeated. It is a novel in the form of variations, which is not so much manipulation of chronology or point of view as it is a disruption between author and narrator. Milan Kundera keeps leaping over his narrator to appear overtly in the stories. It is in *Laughter and Forgetting* that Kundera moves back and forth from the historical to the fantastic, where previously introduced motifs and fantastic events are brought together with real facts. (We think of Marquez's magical realism here, and the broader connection between Central Europe and Latin American literature in our era.) As Lodge has said: "The outrages of modern history in those regimes are of such a scale that only the 'overt lie' of the fantastic and the grotesque can represent them."

It is in both *The Book of Laughter and Forgetting* and *The Unbearable
Lightness of Being* that Kundera clearly portrays history as a narrated story,
and shows the fabrication of what is called the truth, or shows history as an
interpretation. In the more recent novel, Kundera's most philosophical novel
to date, he considers such questions as individual responsibility, Nietzsche's
'eternal return,' and chance and coincidence in life. Again, familiar motifs are
here: erotic trickery in order to outwit fate, self deception, the limits of
human lucidity, and the games of history. The now-familiar technique of
mixing history and the fantastic is rampant in this story. The characters have
a goal of making decisions, but, since Kundera rejects Nietzsche's eternal
return, his characters cannot learn from repeated events, and thus, decisions
or actions cannot weigh heavily on them. We are, like his characters, relieved
of that responsibility of learning from history. Robert interprets Kundera's
sense of "lightness of being" in this way: "If reality were like clockwork,
history would have been infinitely organized. Any accident would have
affected the whole: there would have to be individual responsibility in
history." If individuals are as light and meaningless as historical events, if
individuals have no responsibility for these events (as Kundera's narrator
suspects in this novel) then how can we determine who we are, where we fit
into the scheme of society's fate, its progress, its demise? Kundera jumps into
his novel to tell us that history is as light as an individual's life. In fact, as early
as 1958, Kundera would write [in "Quelque part la derriere," *Le debat*, Vol 8,
January, 1981, pp. 50-63]:

> ... les mé canismes psychologiques qui fonctionnent dans les
> grands é vénements historiques (apparemment incroyables et
> inhumains) sont les mêmes qui régissent les situations in times
> (toutà fait banales et humaines.).

> [... the psychological mechanisms which function in the grand
> (and apparently inhuman and unbelievable) historic events are
> the same which rule intimate (and completely banal and human)
> situations.].

Whether readers understand the novel's quartet of Tereza, Tomas,
Sabina and Franz as representing weightiness or lightness, (or probably, as
structures or variations on a theme), it is clear that Kundera's fictional mode
is now more philosophical than political. He uses Nietzsche as an
introduction to Tomas's philosophical quandary between weightiness and
lightness, and the reader is led through the philosophical maze of questions

concerning individual identity in this world either devoid of individual responsibility or filled to overflowing with personal responsibility. Tomas keeps fluctuating between the negation of both social and personal responsibility, and accepting the burden of Teresa's ponderous love, his country's shame, and his medical work (where he, as a surgeon, claims to be able to find another's identity with the act of cutting open another's body). Tomas finally chooses the responsibility of another's life (weightiness), marries Teresa and moves to a farm commune, and thus has his identity given to him by his circumstances. By Kundera's ironic slight of hand, however, Tomas has also managed to choose lightness of being: he has moved from city to simple country life; he has given up a very controlled medical profession (the weightiness of his beloved work); and, he is now free and away from authorities, living a simpler, rather idyllic life of limited responsibility, freer to define who he is. Kundera has ended his novel ironically; the reader may choose the philosophical stance he prefers as he finishes the novel. Has the protagonist found an identity, or given up the search?

After having looked at Kundera's oeuvre in terms of his being solidly based in the post-modern intellectual camp, it would be beneficial to digress briefly for the purpose of coming at a conclusion from another angle. The original question of this investigation was: How does Milan Kundera, who is solidly post-modern in his theoretical stance and in his fiction, who espouses a modernist (some say, nihilistic or anti-humanist) credo of lack of certainties in life, lack of high tragedy in human events, how does this very modern writer manage to convey the bittersweet beauty inherent in the sometimes absurd, often meaningless lives in his books? How does he successfully shun, as R. C. Porter claims he does, both the literature of incoherence and the literature of absolute ideas? The following brief digression is meant to put his seemingly janus-faced contribution into an historical context.

First of all, intellectuals from Central Europe have always been engaged, have always had an ethical motivation for their theoretical output. The charges of an "arid formalism or political escapism" which members of literature departments level against post-modern theoreticians are just not applicable to Slavic writers. "In the Slavic world, structuralism is seen not as the cerebral play of a few armchair theoreticians, but as a clear-cut political stance...." For Kundera, whose nostalgia yearns for the Bohemia of pre-history, who sees his whole oeuvre [in "Un occident kidnappé," *Le debat*, Vol. 27, November, 1983, pp. 3-22], "comme une longue méditation sur le fin possible de l'humanité européene" [as a long meditation on the possible end of European civilization], literary theory must be attached to the ethical; and, in fact, the importance of this art (modern literature from Prague, Budapest or Warsaw) does not lie in the fact that it criticizes this or that political regime, but "that it offers new testimony about mankind in a social or political setting which people here in the West cannot even imagine" [Kundera, "Comedy Is Everywhere," *Index on Censorship*, Vol. 6, November/December, 1977].

Secondly, even Jacques Derrida admits to an ethical, even political thrust of modern literary theory when he writes in *Écriture et la différence* that the only way to do battle with Western metaphysical absolutism is through stratagem or strategy. Sounding particularly political, he suggests playing a "double game" or double agent, "serving two sides" or feigning obedience to a system of rule while simultaneously trying to undermine its rule by posing unsolvable problems. He continues: "The question here is to pretend to speak the master's language in order to kill him." This sounds like the strategy of any minority, and defeated group (i.e., Kundera's citizens in post-1969 occupied Czechoslovakia). The key to keeping one's identity intact is that "arriére pensée," a mental reservation, held back so that one does not buy into the ideology completely. Kundera calls it a moment of pause before we give an arbitrary significance to a word. So, Derrida concludes, modern theories need not be so alienated from ethical concerns; they can be, on the contrary, "active interventions." An artist need not be enclosed in some "prison house of language," but rather engaged in very political, ethical pursuits. Milan Kundera elegantly makes that bridge or crossover from aesthetics to ethics, and his motivation is clear in this borrowed quote from a 1983 article: "Only in opposing history can you oppose today's history." By questioning an individual's responsibility in historical events, the individual can better define his responsibility and his essence in contemporary events.

Francois Lyotard, author of *The Post-Modern Condition* and several other texts considering that state of contemporary knowledge, has said that post-modern knowledge refines our sensitivity to differences and reinforces our ability to tolerate the incommensurable. Milan Kundera's work is a product of this post-scientific era, an era, according to Lyotard, in which narrative knowledge will be more valuable to us than scientific knowledge. Since, according to most post-modern theorists, language is no longer a system of signs, but "tricks or games," or, to quote Jameson's forward to this text, "a conflictual relationship between tricksters," Kundera's themes of linguistic and historical trickery of sleight of hand are definitely post-modern. But also, Kundera shares with these new theorists the goal of generating new ideas, new kinds of knowledge, and ultimately, a new way of looking at man. Kundera's art offers a way of seeking one's identity in this post-modern world of extremes. He suggests, in his novels, another alternative—beyond those of nihilism or absolute truth.

Each age has its dominant way of the sign, and the things they signify, says Foucault in *The Archeology of Knowledge*. Lyotard, in *The Post-Modern Condition*, claims that there are scientific periods of history, but now, there is a revival of the narrative view of truth. He insists that scientific knowledge is based on narrative truth anyway, that theories are just disguised narratives, that philosophy too was just a seductive tale. He gives as examples Plato's "Myth of the Cave," a non-scientific narrative used to inaugurate science, or Descartes resorting to what he calls the "story of the mind" in his *Discourses* or even Aristotle suggesting that scientific knowledge is composed only of arguments (i.e., dialectics). For Lyotard, narrative is not just a new field of research, but a mode of thinking, fully as legitimate as that of abstract logic.

Another urgent level of Lyotard's text proposes that the narrative must generate the illusion of an imaginary resolution of real contradictions. It is on this level that a real correspondence between Kundera and Lyotard can be made: using as his backdrop real contradictions, (social, political and historical), Kundera creates illusions (a fiction) of imaginary resolutions, or he emphasizes the imaginary aspects of his resolutions. That, then, is another function of mixing the fantastic with the real in these novels. The very idea of "idyll" on which Kundera relies so often, is his "illusion of a resolution." Carlos Fuentes calls Kundera's notion of idyll, "a Communist offering to forget the past, a false remembering." His characters are desperately looking back (into prehistory?), through the memory of "old signs" to find themselves. It is this concept of idyll that will be exploited to suggest a dreamy, almost mythic, remembering of early Moravian folk culture as sedative to the barrage of absurdities in the post-modern world. Kundera defines idyll this way in *The Unbearable Lightness of Being*:

"... an image ... like a memory of Paradise" or "... a looking back to Paradise." But, Kundera's ultimate message is that the good old days cannot return because there never was an original, or a model to imitate. The concept of an original is only a disabled metaphor. The narrative, or history, had always already begun, and it changed a little each time in the telling, so now history is a story that never ends. What is myth, but a collection of stories endlessly retold, and Lyotard would add that all discourse is narrative, so really we live in an age when reason or truth is transformed into mythos (myth) and thus all history is myth.

Many of Kundera's contemporaries in Czechoslovakia see him portraying Central Europe as "a Europe raped by Asia ... a spiritual grave-yard maintained by governments of forgetting," and his idea of history as an "inexhaustible store of cruel jokes." For [Vaclav] Havel, Kundera's history is a "deity capable of deceiving and destroying us, playing tricks on us," and thus real life is elsewhere, outside of history. Real life, for Kundera as well as for other post-modern theorists like Lyotard, is in myth, or in narration, or in interpretation.

In 1964, Kundera wrote *The Joke*, a cult book for the intelligentsia in Czechoslovakia, and the book that resulted in his expulsion from his homeland and emigration to France. This early novel seems to embody his later themes of history as myth and, at the same time, to provide the rationale for proclaiming Kundera as a modern humanist. The novel deals with folk culture and prehistory in an absurd environment. Ludvic, a clever university student, sends a post-card to his girlfriend (a passionate Stalinist), and as a joke says, "optimism is the opium of the people ... long live Trotsky." The result is his expulsion from the university and the Party, and years of labor in the mines. Years later, after a completely unsatisfactory life as a result of that one joke, he is in his hometown, and witnesses the legendary "Ride of the Kings," a folk tradition that will illustrate to him "our world of ever-accelerating forgetting." He writes:

> Suddenly I saw it all clearly. People willingly deceive themselves with a double false faith. They believe in eternal memory (of men, deeds, things) ... and in rectification (of deeds, errors, sins, injustice). Both are shams. The truth lies at the opposite end of the scale: everything will be forgotten, and nothing will be rectified. All rectification will be taken over by oblivion. No one will rectify wrongs; all wrongs will be forgotten.

While watching the "Ride of the Kings," however, Kundera's narrator (whose son was chosen to be this year's King in the parade) reflects on the origin of the legend of the King's Ride:

> Where did it come from and what does it mean? Does it perhaps date back to pagan times ... The "Ride of the Kings" is a mysterious rite; no one knows what it signifies, what its message is ... perhaps the Ride of Kings is beautiful to us at least partly because the message it was meant to communicate has long been

lost, leaving the gestures, colors, and words to stand out all the more clearly.

It is in Moravia, Kundera's ancestral land, where he:

> had the sensation of hearing verse in the most primitive sense of the word, the kind of verse I could never hear on the radio or on TV ... it was a sublime and polyphonic music—each of the heralds declaimed his verse in a monotone, but each on his own individual note, so the voices combined willy-nilly into chords.

This music of variation describes also Kundera's technique of theme building already noted. Kundera's sense of myth (of history as myth), which his protagonist seems to find in his folk culture, is the key to his love of humanity. Perhaps he believes it is futile to seek to shape the future, or to recapture the past, but it is in these rare moments when his characters fall back beyond history into myth, that Kundera reveals his own nostalgia for human solidarity, some common past which is an amalgam of truth and legend. The narrator's thoughts, while playing the final folk concert after the "Ride of the Kings" is played out, are moving. He says, "I felt a long-forgotten sense of companionship come over me." He and three friends are playing in a noisy cafe filling up with a young, boisterous audience; but, says the narrator:

> We managed to forget what was going on around us and create a magic circle of music; it was like being walled off from the drunks in a glass cabin at the bottom of the sea ... I felt happy inside of the songs ... where sorrow wasn't playful, laughter wasn't mocking, love wasn't laughable ... where love is still love, pain, pain and values free from devastation.

This a rare instance, among all of Kundera's novels, where the author describes a freedom from irony, where the author feels no irony, and this instance is in myth, in Kundera's rediscovery of his folk culture. This is Kundera's nostalgia, his own kitsch, his own way of forgetting history—through folk tradition, legend or myth. Predictably, however, he immediately counters with:

> I was equally aware that my home was not of this world ... that everything we sang and played was only a memory, a monument,

a recreation in images of something that no longer was, and I felt
the firm ground of my homeland sinking under my feet, felt
myself falling ... into the depths where love is love and pain, pain,
and I said to myself that my only real home was this descent, this
searching eager fall, and I gave myself up to it, savoring the
sensuous vertigo.

Here is Kundera, the master of "epicurean accommodation"; he has chosen
accommodation to an absurd world, not denial or revolt, and he is instantly
a post-modern writer. For an instant, I think, we see what is the core of his
attraction for modern readers, why he is not a nihilist, why he is not an
ideologue. It is his method of accommodation to modern angst.

In his choice of accommodation, Kundera leaves room for the
importance of the individual; while institutions and political systems may be
absurd, individuals are not. In *The Unbearable Lightness of Being*, Kundera is
constantly studying individual life, how concrete it is, how varied it is, how
beautiful it can be. Most of his characters in this novel have no outside
system of reference, so they must constantly make decisions. Human life is
celebrated in this novel in all its chaotic progress, and, as Robert has
described it, in all its existential contingency. The protagonist's life turns on
coincidences; the very beauty of life, however, is in these coincidences.

The characters in this novel live in a non-tragic mode of fiction, in
their own brand of twentieth-century folk culture. Kundera sees his
characters as central European, representing the flip-side of European
history, its outsiders, its victims. It is this historical disenchantment which is
the source of their non-tragic character which "se moque de la grandeur et
de la gloire" [mocks grandeur and glory]. In Kundera's post-Stalinist Central
Europe there are few of the elements of high tragedy like grandeur, high
status, or fatal flaw, so it is understandable that what is left is a sense of
humor, a sense of humor which allows one to see other points of view, and to
seek a measure of values on a human scale. But Kundera also finds beauty in
man's sense of discomfort in the modern ideological world. Fuentes explains
that while "Central Europe took care to demonstrate that a man need not be
an insect in order to be treated as such," there is, when one reads Kundera,
a change in Kafka's scenario: "The cockroach no longer thinks he knows;
now he knows he thinks." He suggests that even if the future has already
taken place and it stinks, maybe the answer for Kundera is "an internal
utopia," a real space of untouchable life. Herein may lie the core of his
constant preoccupation with sex and love. Kundera wrote in *The Book of
Laughter and Forgetting*:

The symphony is a musical epic. We might compare it to a journey leading through the boundless reaches of the external world, on and on, farther and farther. Variations also constitute a journey, but not through the external world. You recall Pascal's pensee about how man lives between the abyss of the infinitely large and the infinitely small. The journey of the variation form leads to that second infinity, the infinity of internal variety concealed in all things.

While there is nothing new in this approach to modern life, Kundera is fresh in his ability to see beauty in our very post-modern condition: the common folk, be he comrade, poet, peasant or professor, swimming in a disconnected world, uncertain of its past, of what is its real present, wallowing sometimes in irony, reveling in coincidence. It is Kafka sans insects, with flesh and blood characters in a modern communist society, striving for some sense of joy and vitality. His is neither the literature of incoherence, nor the fiction of ideology. He is capable of satirizing loss of memory, but still offering unlimited possibilities of choices to his characters. He talks about the "semantic hoax" by which the same word can be endowed with the opposite meaning, or with a meaning just a little off, the same successive approximations which he and Lyotard and Derrida use to describe communication in general. I suppose we are talking here about a metonymic and not a metaphoric relation (an associational and not an exact correspondence), and that it applies to Kundera's treatment of historic truth, meaning in language, and possibilities of knowing. Kundera's very ethical goal [according to Carlos Fuentes] seems to be to "discover the yet unknown avenues that depart from history and lead us to realities we had hardly suspected." What is pleasing about this goal is that it celebrates our very post-modern condition; instead of wallowing in the hopelessness of it all, it celebrates our very lack of connection to external codes, to institutions, and heralds the yet unknown possibilities for men—unconnected, demystified, and deconstructed. Kundera's (and Derrida's and Lyotard's) contribution might be as simple as the suggestion that the invariable is only one way of looking at things, that others do exist. Perhaps Kundera's folk culture offers not a collision with these post-modern forces, but an instance of beautiful accommodation.

Chronology

1929	Born on April 1, in Brno, Czechoslovakia, to the pianist and musicologist Ludvik Kundera and Milada Janosikova Kundera.
1948	Leaves Brno to study script writing and directing at the Film Faculty of the Prague Academy of Music and Dramatic Arts.
1952	Begins teaching cinematography at the Prague Academy.
1953	Publishes his first poetry collection *Clovek, zahrada sira (Man: A Broad Garden)*.
1955	Publishes *Posledni maj (The Last May)*.
1957	Publishes *Monology (Monologues)*.
1961	Publishes *Unemi romanu*, a critical study of Czechoslovakian novelist Vladislava Vancury.
1962	Publishes his first play, *Majitele klicu (The Owners of the Keys)*.
1963	Begins serving on the Central Committee of the Czechoslovak Writers Union, and on the editorial boards of the journals *Literarni noviny* and *Listy*.
1967	After battling the censorship board for two years, his first novel *Zert (The Joke)* is published. Later that year, speaking in the opening ceremonies at the Fourth Czechoslovakian Writers Congress, he admonishes censorship.

1968	Publishes *Laughable Loves*, a collection of short stories. Russian military forces invade Czechoslovakia. Kundera is expelled from the Communist Party, released from his teaching position at the Prague Academy, and his works are removed from libraries and bookstores.
1973	Publishes his second novel, *Life Is Elsewhere*, in Paris. Wins the Prix Medicis for the best foreign novel published in France.
1975	Leaves Czechoslovakia and accepts an offer to teach comparative literature at the University of Rennes in France.
1979	Following the publication of *The Book of Laughter and Forgetting*, the Czechoslovakian government revoked his citizenship.
1980	Accepts a professorship at the Ecole des hautes etudes en sciences sociales in Paris.
1981	Receives the Commonwealth Award for distinguished service in literature.
1982	Receives the Prix Europa for literature.
1983	Receives an Honarary Doctorate from University of Michigan.
1984	Publishes *The Unbearable Lightness of Being* and receives the Los Angeles Times Book Prize for fiction.
1985	Receives the Jerusalem Prize for Literature on the Freedom of Man in Society.
1987	Receives the Academie Francaise critics prize and the Nelly Sachs prize.
1988	*The Unbearable Lightness of Being* is adapted for film.
1990	Publishes *Immortality*.
1991	Receives the *Independent* Award for foreign fiction.
1994	Publishes *La Lenteur (Slowness)*.
1996	Publishes *Identity*.
2000	Publishes *Art of the Novel*.
2002	Publishes *Ignorance*.

Contributors

HAROLD BLOOM is Sterling Professor of the Humanities at Yale University and Henry W. and Albert A. Berg Professor of English at the New York University Graduate School. He is the author of over 20 books, including *Shelley's Mythmaking* (1959), *The Visionary Company* (1961), *Blake's Apocalypse* (1963), *Yeats* (1970), *A Map of Misreading* (1975), *Kabbalah and Criticism* (1975), *Agon: Toward a Theory of Revisionism* (1982), *The American Religion* (1992), *The Western Canon* (1994), and *Omens of Millennium: The Gnosis of Angels, Dreams, and Resurrection* (1996). *The Anxiety of Influence* (1973) sets forth Professor Bloom's provocative theory of the literary relationships between the great writers and their predecessors. His most recent books include *Shakespeare: The Invention of the Human*, a 1998 National Book Award finalist, and *How to Read and Why*, which was published in 2000. In 1999, Professor Bloom received the prestigious American Academy of Arts and Letters Gold Medal for Criticism.

ROBERT C. PORTER has been an English educator specializing in Russian Literature. His published work includes *Milan Kundera: A Voice from Central Europe*.

PEARL K. BELL has been a critic and an essayist who has written widely about literature and life. Her work has appeared in such journals as *Commentary* and *The New Leader*.

PETER KUSSI has been a professor of Slavic languages and literature at Columbia University. He has been the editor of such books as *Toward the Radical Center, a Karel Capek Reader* and *Writing on the Wall: An Anthology of Czech Literature*.

JOHN BAYLEY is a prominent essayist, novelist and literary scholar. He was married to the novelist Iris Murdoch, and has recently published two books about her life: *Iris: A Memoir* and *Iris and Her Friends*.

MARK STURDIVANT is a literary scholar and essayist. His work has appeared in *Critique* and *Short Story Criticism*.

ROGER KIMBALL has been the Managing Editor of *The New Criterion*. He is the author of *Tenured Radicals: How Politics Has Corrupted Our Higher Education*.

TERRY EAGLETON has been called the premiere British Marxist literary critic. His published works include *The Significance of Theory* and *Heathcliff and the Great Hunger*.

ITALO CALVINO was one of Italy's most celebrated writers. His intelligent and imaginative fiction and essays have been translated and read worldwide. His publications include *If on a Winter's Night a Traveler, The Castle of Crossed Destinies* and *The Baron in the Trees*.

ELLEN PIFER has been a professor of Modern & Contemporary Literature & Culture and Comparative Literature. Her publications include *Demon or Doll: Images of the Child in Contemporary Writing and Culture* and *Saul Bellow Against the Grain*, which received *Choice* magazine's Outstanding Academic Book Award for 1990-91.

JAMES S. HANS has been a professor of English at Wake Forest University. He is the author of numerous books, including *The Play of the World, The Value(s) of Literature* and *The Mysteries of Attention*.

MICHAEL CARROLL is a writer and a literary scholar whose literary essays have appeared in the volume *Milan Kundera and the Art of Fiction* and in the journal *Short Story Criticism*.

JOHN O'BRIEN has held fellowships at the University of Iowa and Stanford University. His work has appeared in *Hudson Review, TriQuarterly* and *Country Journal.* He is the author of *At Home in the Heart of Appalachia.*

TOM WILHELMUS has been the Chair of the Indiana Humanities Council, and has taught in the English department at the University of Southern Indiana in Evansville. His work has appeared in such journals as *Hudson Review.*

VICKI ADAMS is a literary scholar and essayist. She has studied the work of writers from Europe, Latin America and the Caribbean. Her work appeared in the volume of essays entitled *Imagination, Emblems and Expressions: Essays on Latin American, Caribbean, and Continental Culture and Identity.*

Bibliography

Aji, Aron, ed. *Milan Kundera and the Art of Fiction: Critical Essays*. New York: Garland Publishing, 1992.

Banerjee, Maria Nemcove. *Terminal Paradox: The Novels of Milan Kundera*. New York: Grove Weidenfeld, 1990.

Baranczak, Stanislaw. "Life Is Elsewhere," *The New Republic*, Vol. 205, No. 5 (July, 1991).

Bayley, John. "Fictive Lightness, Fictive Weight," *Salmagundi*, Vol. 73 (Winter, 1987): 84-92.

Caldwell, Ann Stewart. "The Intrusive Narrative Voice of Milan Kundera," *Review of Contemporary Fiction 9*, No. 2 (Summer, 1989): 46-52.

Cooke, Michael. "Milan Kundera: Cultural Arrogance and Sexual Tyranny," *Critical Survey* 4, No. 1 (1992): 79-84.

Dolezel, Lubomir. *Narrative Modes in Czech Literature*. Toronto: University of Toronto Press, 1973.

French, A. *Czech Writers and Politics: 1945-1969*. Boulder: East European Monographs, No. XCIV, 1982.

Fuentes, Carlos. "The Other K," *Triquarterly* 51 (1981): 268.

Gaugham, Richard T. "Man Thinks; God Laughs": Kundera's "Nobody Will Laugh," *Studies In Short Fiction*, Vol. 29, No. 1 (Winter, 1992).

Goetz-Stankiewicz, Marketa. *The Silenced Theatre: Czech Playwrights without a Stage*. Toronto: University of Toronto Press, 1979.

Gopinathan Pillai, C. *The Political Novels of Milan Kundera and O.V. Vijayan: A Comparative Study*. Prestige, 1996.

Gray, Paul. "Broken Circles." *Time* 116, No. 24 (15 December 1980): 89.

Kiebuzinska, Christine. *Jacques and His Master: Kundera's Dialogue with Diderot.* *Comparative Literature Studies*, Vol. 29, No. 1 (1992).

Kundera, Milan. "The Novel and Europe." *New York Review of Books 19* (July, 1984): 15.

———. "The Making of a Writer," *New York Book Review* 24 (October, 1982): 37.

Liehm, Antonin J. *The Politics of Culture*, translation from the Czech by Peter Kussi. New York: Grove, 1972.

———. "Milan Kundera: Czech Writer," *Czech Literature since 1955: A Symposium.* Eds. William E. Harkins and Paul I. Trensky. New York: Bohemica Press, 1980.

Lindroth, Colette. "Mirrors of the Mind: Kaufman Conquers Kundera," *Literature/Film Quarterly* Vol. 19, No. 4 (1991): 229-234.

Lodge, David. "From Don Juan to Tristan." *Times Literary Supplement*, No. 4234 (25 May, 1984): 567-68.

Medwich, Cathleen. "People are Talking about ... Milan Kundera." *Vogue* 171, No. 2 (February 1981): 260-61, 330-31.

McEwan, Ian. "An Interview with Milan Kundera," *Granata* 11 (1984): 34-35.

Misurella, Fred. *Understanding Milan Kundera: Public Events, Private Affairs.* Columbia: University of South Carolina Press, 1993.

Moore, Susan. "Kundera: The Massacre of Culture," *Quadrant.* (April, 1987): 63-66.

O'Brien, John. *Dangerous Intersections: Milan Kundera and Feminism.* New York: St. Martin's Press, 1995.

Petro, Peter, ed. *Critical Essays on Milan Kundera.* New York: Twayne Publishers, 1999.

———. "Apropos Dostoevsky: Brodsky, Kundera and the Definition of Europe." *Literature and Politics in Central Europe: Studies in Honour of Marketa Goetz-Stankiewicz*, ed. Leslie Miller, Klaus Peterson, Peter Stenberg, and Karl Zaenker, pp. 76-90. Columbia: Camden House, 1993.

Pichova, Hana. "The Narrator in Milan Kundera's *The Unbearable Lightness of Being*," *Slavic and East European Journal.* Vol. 36, No. 2 (1992): 217-226.

Plimpton, George, ed. "Writers at Work: *The Paris Review*," *Interviews, 6th Series*. New York: Viking Penguin Press, 1986.

Porter, Robert. *Milan Kundera: A Voice from Central Europe*. Denmark: Arkona Press, 1981.

Restuccia, Frances L. *"Homo Homini Lupus:* Milan Kundera's *The Joke."* *Contemporary Literature 31*, No. 3 (Fall 1990): 281-99.

Ricard, Francois. "Satan's Point of View." Trans. John Anzalone, *Salmagundi 73*. (Winter 1987): 58-64.

_____. "The Fallen Idyll: A Rereading of Milan Kundera." *Review of Contemporary Fiction 9*, No. 2 (Summer 1989): 17-26.

Roth, Philip. *Reading Myself and Others*. New York: Farrar, Straus, 1975.

Sanders, Ivan. "Mr. Kundera, the European," *The Wilson Quarterly*. (Spring, 1991).

Stavans, Ilan. *"Jacques and His Master:* Kundera and His Precursors." *Review of Contemporary Fiction 9*, No. 2 (Summer 1989): 88-96.

Trensky, Paul I. *Czech Drama since World War II*. New York: M.E. Sharpe Publishers, 1978.

Vejvoda, Serge. "Kundera's *Immortality* The Sneak Foretaste." *San Francisco Review* XV, No. 4 (Spring 1991): 6, 12.

von Kunes, Karen. "The National Paradox: Czech Literature and the Gentle Revolution." *World Literature Today 65*, No. 2 (Spring 1991): 237-40.

Webb, Igor. "Milan Kundera and the Limits of Scepticism," *The Massachusetts Review*. Vol. XXXI, No. 3 (Autumn 1990): 357-368.

Acknowledgments

"'Freedom is my Love': The Works of Milan Kundera" by Robert C. Porter. The article was originally published in *Index on Censorship*, Winter 1975: pp. 41-6. © 1975 by *Index on Censorship*. For more information, visit *Index* on the web at www.indexoncensorship.org.

"The Real Avante-Garde" by Pearl K. Bell. © 1980 by *Commentary*. Reprinted from *Commentary*, December 1980, by permission; all rights reserved.

"Milan Kundera: Dialogues with Fiction" by Peter Kussi. From *World Literature Today*, Vol. 57, No. 2, (1983): 206-09. © 1983 by *World Literature Today*. Reprinted by permission.

"Kundera and Kitsch" by John Bayley. This article first appeared in the *London Review of Books*, Vol. 6, No. 10, (June, 1984): 18-19, © 1984 by *London Review of Books*. Reprinted by permission of *London Review of Books*, web address: www.lrb.cu.uk.

"Milan Kundera's Use of Sexuality" by Mark Sturdivant. From *Critique: Studies in Modern Fiction*, Vol. XXVI, No. 3, (Spring, 1985): 131-40. Reprinted with permission of the Helen Dwight Reid Educational Foundation. Published by Heldref Publications, 1319 Eighteenth St., NW, Washington, DC 20036-1802. Copyright © 1985

"The Ambiguities of Milan Kundera" by Roger Kimball. From *The New Criterion*, Vol. IV, No. 5, (1986): 5-13. © 1986 by *The New Criterion*. Reprinted by permission.

"Estrangement and Irony" by Terry Eagleton. From *Salmagundi*, No. 73, (Winter, 1987): 25-32. © 1987 by *Salmagundi*. Reprinted by permission.

"On Kundera" by Italo Calvino. From *Review of Contemporary Fiction*, Vol. 9, No. 2, (1989): 53-7. © 1989 by *Review of Contemporary Fiction*. Reprinted by permission.

"The Book of Laughter and Forgetting: Kundera's Narration against Narration" by Ellen Pifer. From *Journal of Narrative Technique*, Vol. 22, No. 2, (Spring, 1992): 84-96. © 1992 by *Journal of Narrative Technique*. Reprinted by permission.

"Kundera's Laws of Beauty" by James S. Hans. From *Essays in Literature*, Vol. XIX, No. 1, (Spring, 1992): 144-58. © 1992 by *Essays in Literature*. Reprinted by permission.

Copyright 1992. From *Milan Kundera and the Art of Fiction*, ed. Aron Aji: 132-52. Reproduced by permission of Routledge, Inc., part of Taylor & Francis Group.

"Milan Kundera: Meaning, Play, and the Role of the Author" by John O'Brien. From *Critique: Studies in Modern Fiction*, Vol. XXIV, No. 1, (Fall, 1992): 3-18. Reprinted with permission of the Helen Dwight Reid Educational Foundation. Published by Heldref Publications, 1319 Eighteenth St., NW, Washington, DC 20036-1802. Copyright © 1992.

"Time and Distance" by Tom Wilhelmus. From *The Hudson Review*, Vol. XLVI, No. 1, (Spring, 1993): 247-55. © 1978 by *The Hudson Review*. Reprinted by permission.

"Milan Kundera: The Search for Self in a Post-Modern World" by Vicki Adams. From *Imagination, Emblems and Expressions: Essays on Latin American, Caribbean, and Continental Culture and Identity*, ed. Helen Ryan-Ranson, 1993: 233-46. © 1993 by Bowling Green State University Popular Press. Reprinted by permission.

Index